17.96

DISCARDED

LEADING
WITH
LOVE

HOW WOMEN AND MEN CAN TRANSFORM THEIR ORGANIZATIONS THROUGH MATERNALISTIC MANAGEMENT

KATHLEEN SANFORD

VASHON PUBLISHING ✦ OLALLA, WASHINGTON

LEADING WITH LOVE: HOW WOMEN (AND MEN) CAN TRANSFORM
THEIR ORGANIZATIONS THROUGH MATERNALISTIC MANAGEMENT
© 1998 by Vashon Publishing

Book design by Sara Patton, Maui, Hawaii
Printed in the United States

PUBLISHER'S CATALOGING-IN-PUBLICATION
(Provided by Quality Books)

Sanford, Kathleen D.
    Leading with love: how women (and men) can transform
their organizations through maternalistic management / by
Kathleen D. Sanford — 1st ed.
    p. cm.
    Includes bibliographical references and index.
    Preassigned LCCN: 97-91352
    ISBN: 0-9661753-7-9

    1. Leadership. 2. Leadership in women. 3. Management
— Philosophy. 4. Organizational behavior.   I. Title.

HD57.7.S36 1998   658.4'094
                                         QBI98-35

This book is dedicated to my mother, JoAlice Robertson Smith. She lived only 26 years and yet was able to leave with me an understanding of maternal nurturance and love to last a lifetime.

Contents

$\mathcal{P}$reface

This book has been twenty years in the making. Ten years ago, the basic concepts were in my head. Five years ago, I started talking about the book's title and about why such a book needed to be written. A year ago, I began writing. But for twenty years I dealt with bosses: my own bosses, bosses who were colleagues, bosses who worked for me. I completed three degrees in management (a Masters in Human Resources Management, a Masters in Business Administration, and a Doctorate in Business Administration). I learned theory, participated in research, and lived life in corporations, all the time knowing I would need to write this book.

When I first talked about the title, colleagues advised me that it wouldn't sell—particularly not to male managers. My answer: "That's just the point." If managers today aren't willing to look at a different way of relating to workers, if they aren't able to conceive of organizations where those in charge actually bring to their jobs a concern for others, if they can't even consider the idea that they can feel love for their organizations, their products, their employees, and their customers, then those managers' businesses are doomed, just as a society with uncaring leaders is doomed. I believe that there are managers and potential managers who practice loving leadership but who simply haven't put a label to their ethical, caring attitudes and behavior. My hope is that this book will help such leaders to understand and define their management style, and that it will encourage them to nurture their own conscious concern and to foster the development of "management maternalism" in others.

I have been accused of perfectionism, of setting my standards too high when it comes to people in leadership roles. My answer is this: If there are to be standards, why should they be anything less than high? If perfectionism means setting goals for improvement and continually working toward them, I accept the label. If, on the other hand, it's defined as an intolerance for errors, failures, or imperfection, I demur. Love for self and others includes a realistic view of faults, an acceptance of foibles. It also calls for efforts to improve. Standards for leaders aren't higher than the standards for anyone else, they're just specific to the role that managers have chosen. Just as we expect proficiency from a housekeeper or a physician in his or her area of specialization, so should we expect competence from a boss. Given that any person in charge has a strong influence on the working lives of employees, it follows that a manager's leadership qualifications must necessarily include a concern for the well-being of others.

Am I saying that women naturally make better leaders than men? Research does indeed indicate that women have the psychological makeup for a more caring management style, yet this book has not been written from a sexist point of view. (If some of the words I've selected evoke sexual stereotyping, they are not meant to. I have based my vocabulary and pronoun choices upon ease of expression and enhancement of communication.) Between 1975 and 1991, sociologists Margaret Maney Mauni and Ann Beittel of the University of Minnesota studied thousands of male and female senior students. They found that women are consistently more compassionate, less competitive, more interested in helping others, and less materialistic than men. While women have traditionally been associated with the values and behaviors that I (and many transformational leaders) advocate for the future of management, I do not believe that only women can practice loving leadership. Men too can be nurturing, empathic, ethical, expressive, inclusive, cooperative, collaborative, and interested in the growth and success of others.

Just as no person succeeds in life without the help of countless others, nothing is written or produced by a single writer working alone. I can't begin to list everyone who has helped me grow and learn, but I do have some specific acknowledgments to make here. Without the support and love of my partner, editor, and husband, Bill Sanford, this book would never have been finished. Without the early help of my friend and typist, Cris Danielson, it would never have been started.

I'm grateful to my children—Jonathan, Michael, and Stephanie—for teaching me how to be maternal. I appreciate my management professors at Pepperdine University, Pacific Lutheran University, and Nova Southeastern University for sharing with me their theories and experience. I'm thankful for what I have learned and continue to learn from my bosses and colleagues. I owe gratitude to the United States Army, the Washington Army National Guard, and the American Business Women's Association (ABWA), all organizations where I have been mentored in leadership. And, finally, I must express not only my thanks but my admiration and love for my extraordinary management and patient-care team at Harrison Memorial Hospital. The caregivers who return to work day after day to nurture and attend to the needs of others are high on my list of heroes.

An Introduction to Maternalism

I'm a boss. You probably are, too, or you want to be. Of course, you may not call yourself a boss. In this country, there can be some amount of stigma attached to the claiming of that title. In fact, some people seem to consider the admission of being a boss not much better than confessing to a social disease. It's a bit more acceptable to describe yourself as a manager, although that word is beginning to have a less than honorable vernacular definition, too. "Executive" seems to be less offensive, though a bit elitist. More popular is the simple term "leader," and some of today's leadership writers believe we should chuck all titles used to describe those persons in organizations who hold the authority. In the future, they claim, there will be no hierarchy: the outdated practice of management will be replaced with the new role of coordination. All former bosses will be called coordinators.

The Proliferation of New Management Theories

Whatever our titles, those of us who have been placed in positions of organizational responsibility for others are finding plenty of challenges. Our companies are struggling with unprecedented change. We're expected to take the lead in

1

managing that change by transforming our workplaces, empowering our associates (who were once called subordinates), and changing our own outmoded ways of relating to others. Companies (and countries) need great leadership now. Most seem to recognize this, and are busily hiring consultants and trying out the most popular management techniques of the moment. We've sampled, among others, new management styles variously titled "benchmarking," "restructuring," "empowerment," "service quality," "strategic planning," "core competencies," "decentralization," "learning organizations," "transformational leadership," "overhead value analysis," "continuous quality improvement," "management by objective (MBO)," "total quality management (TQM)," and "horizontal and vertical integration." Each new management technique is purported to be the answer, but when it doesn't prove to be the magic bullet in record time, we move on to the next great idea.

I believe that many of these ideas have merit. They appeal to my intuition about what people want in their lives. What leaves me a bit skeptical is the way they're being bought into lock, stock, and barrel. It looks as if many companies are seeking a Pied Piper to lead them merrily forward through rough times to a promised land of milk, honey, and profitability with the least amount of pain. In their eagerness to find a corporate panacea, some leaders import ideas that simply aren't right for their companies. Or they pick the one part of a theory that appeals to them, not discerning whether one segment alone can deliver on its promise, without the entire doctrine being in place. Most discouraging of all, some leaders adopt practices based on more than one theory, even when common sense should tell them that the ideas being implemented are diametrically opposed.

A classic example of this mixed-theory management is the leader who preaches "empowerment" and wants front-line workers to make decisions based on what's good for the company, while at the same time she is explaining that the current layoffs are harbingers of the future — that future where no one really owns a job, where there is no job security, where full-time employees will be replaced by a contingency workforce, where company-worker loyalty is to give way to contractual agreements between corporations and temporary, just-passing-through nonemployees.

What's an employee to think? That he is likely to be a "temp" through no fault of his own. This doesn't encourage him to be familiar with or supportive of the company's mission and goals, and yet the boss wants to empower him with the responsibility for making decisions.

Why are today's companies so receptive to new management theories? Because we recognize the need to improve our workplaces, and we realize that management practices are the key to any improvement. If you are a manager, you are pivotal to the success of your business. As a manager, you probably have a vision of what your company should and could be. One of the great things about being human is our ability to daydream. Through the power of our minds, we're able to escape from current realities by merely closing our eyes and envisioning things the way we think they ought to be. Most of us have dreams for ourselves — imaginative pictures we've drawn of the future we want to inhabit. As managers, we have ideas about how our companies and associates could be, if the world were only perfect. The management techniques we're willing to try are those that promise to help us achieve at least some part of our corporate dreams.

If your management daydreams include a profitable company that has a loyal customer group and a great reputation for quality and service, if you envision skilled, productive employees who take pride in excellence, enjoy coming to work, are able to settle their own interpersonal disputes, and want to share responsibility for the company with the traditional managers, then most of the current management theories will appeal to you. Each has merit because it makes intuitive sense. So why do so many companies fail to make successful use of these theories?

Loving Concern

Great ideas come to naught when they are missing the one crucial component that is essential to long-term success. When theoretical management techniques are applied to a real-life work setting, the thing that will determine their success is a deep, fundamental concern for customers, employees, and the company, similar to the caring of a loving parent. If this loving concern is missing, then techniques taught to increase the company's competitiveness, productivity, profitability, or employee relations—no matter how legitimate—are mere manipulation. They only work for the short term, until those who have been manipulated figure it out.

For many companies, numerous attempts to change by adopting a succession of techniques have resulted in a generation of faltering careers, frustrated managers, and growing cynicism among both the leaders and the followers. And yet some companies are able to boast of huge successes with one or more of these ideas. Why are some organizations able to achieve outstanding results by instituting the very same theories that fail dismally elsewhere? Because they have an underlying set of beliefs that make the difference. Their leadership teams have evolved to a level where they are able to practice the kind of caring management that I call "maternalism."

No, I'm not talking about companies run only by women. In fact, some of the most successful management stories come from organizations led by men known for their competitiveness. The comeback saga of IBM, the continual excellence of Motorola, and the dramatic business turnaround at Harley-Davidson are all examples of loving leadership at work.

Louis V. Gerstner, Jr., Chairman and CEO of the International Business Machines Corporation, might be surprised to hear himself described as a "loving leader." Yet his maternalistic actions, such as supporting a diverse work force, nurturing talent among all of his team, and committing resources to work and family issues, are the foundations for IBM's ascent out of their recent rough times. The restructuring and reduction in force at IBM could have resulted in a disillusioned employee group with decreased productivity and widespread bitterness toward the CEO. Instead, IBM retains worker loyalty, and Gerstner was recognized by *Working Mother* magazine in 1995 as a "corporate leader who has taken personal responsibility for making his or her workplace more family-friendly."

Motorola, Inc., is one of the world's leading manufacturers of pagers, cellular phones, and semiconductors. Its name is synonymous with quality and steady, long-term growth. TQM, benchmarking, empowerment, and re-engineering have all been tried there . . . and they've all worked. In fact, they've worked so well that Motorola is consistently pointed to as a great success story for modern management theories. Why do these concepts work at Motorola? Because of the company's maternalism, as evidenced in its dedication to life-long learning for employees; its development of relationships with customers, suppliers, employees, and community; and its new human resources program, "Lifesteps," with benefits meant to help employees thrive in different life stages—at home as well as on the job.

The vision that comes to mind when one thinks of Harley-Davidson, maker of heavyweight motorcycles, probably isn't maternal. Yet it was a switch to maternalistic tenets that brought about the miraculous comeback of a company whose very existence was threatened in the last decade. Management, working hand in hand with labor, changed the corporate culture to include more trust, openness, and partnership so that the Harley-Davidson "family" could succeed together, and succeed they have.

IBM, Motorola, and Harley-Davidson are just three of a growing number of maternal success stories. They are examples of organizations that are thriving in an age of uncertainty. What sets them apart is that they have figured out the problem with just picking up trendy management practices and plunking them down in a company setting: it doesn't work!

Another problem with most management theories is the tendency to deal with limited components of the business. Each theory emphasizes a different group of stakeholders. There are those that push customer service, those that stress finance or marketing or profitability, those that accent the need for employee job satisfaction and employee relations. Very few address the need for managers to take care of themselves and other managers. Since whatever is focused on determines what is missed, emphasis on any isolated segment of the organizational population means that other segments are neglected. Techniques fail when their practice causes an imbalance in the organization—that is, when all segments are not tended to. Maternalism, in contrast, is a holistic management practice because its emphasis is on balance.

While the characteristics of maternalism have always been associated with the feminine gender, it has been my experience that men, too, can excel at both serving and empowering others. Paternalism has been practiced by both sexes for centuries. Maternalism is an approach that every manager and business should consider adopting if they want not merely to survive, but to thrive, in the future. Male or female, you can transform your organization by:

1. **Understanding how we got to where we are.** Chapter One of this book provides a picture of management as it is viewed today, and introduces the theory of maternalism. Chapter Two gives an overview of management theory, both as it has been practiced in the past and as it is proposed for today and for the future. It also presents a rationale for why

we still need managers. (Rumors of our demise have been greatly exaggerated.)

2. Learning how to really care for an organization. No, company loyalty is not a thing of the past. Chapter Three tells why it can't be if you and your corporation are to thrive. It explains how to live a management life that demonstrates and encourages the love for the company that will be essential for future success.

3. Learning how to really care for the employee team. Chapter Four tells you how to get beyond manipulation by giving to the employees, or associates, what they need and want from management.

4. Learning how to really care for the customers. Good customer service isn't enough. Your future success is directly linked to your true concern for those who buy your products or services. Chapter Five explains what loving the customer is about, and what it looks like.

5. Learning to be a community steward. Chapter Six is a reminder that the organization is a subsystem of the community and has a responsibility to the greater system.

6. Learning how to care for yourself. This is the area most often neglected in management texts. The frustrations, loneliness, and high expectations that go along with leadership positions need to be addressed, so that leaders can avoid becoming burned out and thereby losing their place on the track to success. Managers need special care. Truly thriving means taking care of yourself . . . and your fellow managers. Chapter Seven tells you how.

7. **Developing a maternalistic organization.** Being a loving leader isn't enough. While personal development is important for an individual's career growth, a maternalistic manager who is alone in a paternalistic or other non-maternalistic type of organization won't thrive. He must be supported within an environment in which the managers, their associates, the customers, and the organization can all flourish. Chapter Eight provides the blueprint for establishing and maintaining the Maternalistic Organization—the institution that we can all vote for as most likely to succeed.

One final introductory note: The titles used in this book to describe people who have responsibility for the performance of other people include "manager," "leader," and, yes, even "boss." Speaking for myself, it doesn't matter what you call me. I know that I have important work to do that will help determine the success of my company, my associates, my customers, my community, and myself. And so have you.

What the world stands so much in need of at the present time, and what it will continue to need if it is to endure and increase in happiness, is more of the maternal spirit.

– Ashley Montagu, 1953

Paternalism: A policy or practice of treating or governing people in a fatherly manner, especially by providing for their needs without giving them rights or responsibilities.

– The American Heritage Dictionary, 1992

Maternalism: No definition provided.

– The American Heritage Dictionary, 1992

Maternalism: 1. A way of treating people in a manner that encourages their growth and development, so that they may become their very best, most successful, independent selves. 2. A theory of leadership based on true concern for the well-being of the organization, the employees, the customers, and the leader.

– Kathleen Sanford, 1997

Why Even Consider a Different Way to Lead?

Love: 1. an intense affection . . . an intense emotional attachment . . . a strong enthusiasm . . . the feeling of benevolence, kindness, or brotherhood toward others . . .

– The American Heritage Dictionary, 1992

This is a book about love. No, not the romantic kind so idealized in music, literature, and the visual media. Not the intense fondness that we feel for family or friends. It's about a different kind of caring—one that has been camouflaged in many American organizations, if it is not absent altogether. This book is about an attribute that modern leaders must possess if their companies—and this country—are to thrive into the next century. It's about what ought to be an axiom: that individuals, organizations, and nations need loving leadership. They require leaders who really care about other people, about whatever it is that they produce, and about themselves. In these times of accelerated change, they need such loving leaders more than ever.

In spite of an old TV-Western term that pervades our thinking as well as our language, management theorists have been trying to tell us for decades that workers are not just "hired hands." Employees have a lot of "stuff" attached to those hands, and they bring that stuff to their jobs. Their personal goals, needs, fears, talents, problems, and abilities come to work with them. People want to be cared about. They want to know that they matter. They want to be esteemed by others. They want some control over their lives, and they want to accomplish something that has meaning. Since so much of life is spent in the workplace, it makes perfect sense that these wants should be part of what people hope to receive in exchange for the work they do. Along with the need to be cared about comes a desire to have those who are in power positions — their managers — demonstrate caring. In this book, such caring is described as love.

To speak of leaders who love may seem out of keeping with current paradigms of what is admired in American industry. Financial whiz kids, brilliant entrepreneurs, visionary executives, and hard-charging CEOs aren't typically described as loving; if they were, it would raise a lot of eyebrows. Loving? In business? Business is for, well, *business,* as in "getting down to," as in no-nonsense, as in sober, sincere, professional. It's not for soft, squishy sentimentality, which could very well get in the way of important, unemotional financial decisions. Business means decisions based on *facts,* not on intuition. Emotions are for a person's private life, not for work. Leave feelings and the fulfillment of emotional needs to home life, to the family.

It is this attitude (or thoughtless practice) of the modern business world that has put us where we are today. And where is that? Do we represent the country with the highest

> If there is one thing I have learned in surveying hundreds of workers in blue and white collar professions, it is this: employees feel estranged from their employers.
>
> — Robert Veninga, Ph.D.

productivity in the world? Are we a nation of workers who look forward to going to our jobs? Are we optimistic about the future of our country? Are our management-worker relationships good? Do we feel good about each other?

Surveys of American workers in the 1990s would indicate that the answers to these questions are all negative. In one 1990 study, only 10 percent of survey respondents reported being satisfied with their jobs. The majority felt that America won't be "number one" after the year 2000, and they did not express positive feelings about their business leaders.[1] It appears that "business as usual" is not satisfying to very many people. Discontent, pessimism, skepticism, and negativity seem to be the order of the day. While there may be any number of rational reasons why this is so, past and current business and leadership practices need to be examined for their part in shaping attitudes about work. Evolving business ideas about scientific management, organizational behavior models, and social and psychological theories either have not yet been implemented or have not produced a happy, productive, job-oriented work force. Could this be because

---

[1] Patterson, James and Kim, Peter: *The Day America Told the Truth*, Harper Audio, Dunmore, Pa. 1991.

> *Even though the economy is doing well, the crime rate is falling, and the cold war is over, unease is everywhere.*
>
> – Graham Fysh, THE NEWS TRIBUNE, April 1997

leadership styles and theories are not capable of producing positive outcomes if those who plan, initiate, and administer them don't truly care about their companies, products, and employees? Could loving leadership be the missing ingredient that is needed to bring about real, meaningful, and effective change?

Chilly Days of Change

In the present time, the words we most often hear repeated about our lives seem to be "chaos" and "change." Much of our recent literature points out the manifest truth that change is an ever-increasing fact of modern life. With technological knowledge doubling every seven years, there is no way to stop the acceleration of transitions for individuals, institutions, and society. The uncertainties in this era of change have left many people feeling out of control in a chaotic world.

Psychologist Kurt Lewin's long-taught theory of change[2] is that human beings are "frozen" in a certain way: they are part of a culture that has prescribed customs, attitudes, tradi-

---

[2] Lewin, Kurt: Frontiers in Group Dynamics: Concepts, Methods and Reality in Social Science, Social Equilibrium and Social Change, *Human Relations*, No. I (June, 1947) 5-41.

tions, and patterns of behavior. When a person changes, he "thaws out," makes the changes, and again "refreezes" with a new or altered set of behaviors.

Life, then, is a series of learning experiences resulting in continued freezing, thawing, and refreezing! With the number and rapidity of changes faced by people today, there doesn't seem to be time for a complete chain of cycles: we don't have time to refreeze before the next thaw. The result? Life in today's world can be described as a state of "slush," and those of us who are attempting to survive and thrive in this icy, unformed flux are a generation of slushpuppies!

Slipping through slush doesn't fit well with biological theory on the natural need for stabilization. The human body seeks a state of equilibrium known as homeostasis. It's constantly at work to balance its internal environment amid the taking in of materials and their conversion or elimination. One definition of stress that can lead to illness is anything that disrupts a person's stable equilibrium. While this is a theory of health, often applied to help medical personnel understand how people get sick (when homeostasis is disturbed), it can also help explain why individuals bombarded by constant change, trying to wend their way through slush, may have great difficulty staying mentally and emotionally well. If our bodies seek homeostasis, it may be that we desire "culturalstasis". . . at least for a little while. Living in an unfrozen world is new to many of us, and it's not comfortable. It leaves us frightened, unsettled, unsure of our place. It causes us to look around for helpers—leaders—to help guide or, at the very least, support us through these slippery, uncertain times.

The Need for Heroes

Since change is affecting every aspect of living, we look for leaders in all arenas. What national political figure can we turn to as the United States is proclaimed the only super-power in a world of trade imbalances, regional warfare, and a global economy? Who can help us figure out solutions to hunger, poverty, illiteracy, our aging infrastructure, our aging population? Who will solve the problems of crime, high taxes, and the deterioration of the environment? As many members of society have begun to question age-old religious and family beliefs, who can help us sort out what we should now believe?

At the personal and economic level, who can help us understand what is happening to our companies? Who can assure us that we will have a way to support ourselves when our current skills become obsolete? Who is working to ensure that we'll even have jobs? Who can be our corporate heroes?

It is said that Americans love heroes. We look for them, both in the national arena and in our personal lives. Our heroes have great strength and ability or unusual courage and purpose. Somehow, they have accomplished feats impossible for the "ordinary" person. We choose to endow them with superhuman attributes. We speak of "hero worship," which seems apropos because most of the world's great religions have been founded upon devotion to divine heroes.

We seek heroes in our social, political, spiritual, and everyday lives. We invent them in fiction. We see them in our history; our belief in their heroism varying according to our own individual views of the world. Sometimes we expect heroic behavior based simply on someone's position in life.

We are sadly disappointed when we don't see heroism where we expect it, just as we have become cynical with the knowledge that our historical heroes were not the paragons we may once have believed. Still, we want our heroes, and we want them to hold leadership positions.

Heroes Are Not Always the Same for Everyone

George Washington	Florence Nightingale	Mahatma Gandhi
Thomas Jefferson	Clara Barton	Eddie Rickenbacker
Abraham Lincoln	Lillian Wald	Winston Churchill
Robert E. Lee	Edith Cavell	Charles Lindbergh
Ulysses S. Grant	Susan B. Anthony	Booker T. Washington
Martin Luther King, Jr.	Sacajewea	Margaret Thatcher
Malcolm X	Helen Keller	Elizabeth Cady Stanton
Tecumseh	Eleanor Roosevelt	Harriet Tubman
Cochise	Amelia Earhart	Mother Teresa
Roger Williams	Dorothea Dix	Cesar Chavez
Thomas Paine	Ronald Reagan	Harriet Beecher Stowe
Chief Joseph	Jane Addams	Emma Goldman
The Dalai Lama	Maria Martinez	Sarah Winnemucca

Whether at the conscious or the subconscious level, we are looking harder than ever for heroic figures—for some magical person or persons who can lead us out of chaos or at least point the way. Confused by the lack of "frozen truths," we look for someone who can explain the world to us, give us a sense of security, even think for us. Some people are so eager to follow *someone, anyone* they can trust, that they make choices most of us cannot understand. It may seem incomprehensible that entire groups of people would submit to the leadership of charismatic but culturally maverick figures, to the point of giving up their wealth, their families, and even their lives for them. Yet we can find numerous examples of such seeming gullibility. In recent times there have been Jim Jones and Jonestown,[3] David Koresh and the Branch Davidians,[4] Marshall Applewhite and the Heaven's Gate cult.[5] Such folk heroes are followed with a devotion that society's more mainstream leaders might envy. Which politicians or industry CEOs can claim supporters whose trust in them is so complete that everything the leader says is taken as truth? In fact, many of those who choose to follow what we have labeled "cults" have a distinct distrust for the mainstream's leadership. At least in this regard, cult members may not be much different from the majority of Americans.

This country's faith and trust in conventional leaders is low. How many individuals, if asked to list the five people they most admire, would include their employer or manager? It's more likely that managers would end up on a "least-liked" list. Being a boss is not considered an admirable profession or career (except maybe to professors of management theory, or to other bosses). Bosses are not heroes. The boss is a person who got ahead by climbing on the backs of others or because of his politics and family connections or because she slept

---

[3] Harrary, K.: The Truth About Jonestown, *Psychology Today*, Mar-Apr. 1992.

[4] Linedecker, C.: *Massacre at Waco, Texas: The Shocking Story of Cult Leader David Koresh*. St. Marten's Paperbacks, New York, 1993.

[5] Adler, Eric: Belief is Up There, *Kansas City Star*, Apr. 5, 1997.

> *In real life, very few crimes and next to no murders are committed by businessmen, yet, in a Media Research Center Study, of 214 murderers on television, about 30 percent were business owners or executives.*
>
> — John Carlson, radio talk show host
> and newspaper columnist

her way to the top. He's mean and demanding. She earns a big salary off the sweat and hard work of others. If he's not a cruel taskmaster, he is a buffoon—someone to laugh at (behind his back, of course.) We know this is true because we've learned it since childhood. If our parents weren't complaining about them, we learned about bosses from television sitcoms or newspaper comic strips. From Beetle Bailey's forgetful General Halftrack to Dagwood's Mr. Dithers to Sally Forth's harried supervisor Ralph to Dilbert's self-important pointy-haired boss, they're mean, foolish, pompous, uninformed, or busy figuring out how to take credit for their subordinates' work. Mostly, they're white males who won't give women or minorities a chance to get ahead. If they're females, they're "Queen Bees," unwilling to help other women succeed.

These depictions make it appear that bosses belong to the less admirable side of humanity. When bosses are philanthropists or humanitarians, somehow their contributions are less valuable than those of the workers they supervise or support. A nurse caring for a hospital patient is noble; the hospital administrator is not. A missionary is noble; the CEO of the company that donated the missionary's equipment is not. Our culture's picture of the Boss is not a flattering portrait.

If television is indicative of the viewing public's attitudes and beliefs, then evidently we expect the very worst of business executives. But, before we start to pity the poor, misunderstood, underappreciated bosses of America, it would be prudent for us to reflect on how they got their reputations. Setting aside the human factor of jealousy for their success, the boss's image as a bad guy is based, in part, on true tales of the past and present.

History is replete with stories of people who have misused their power over others. Kings, warlords, and chieftains have used their positions to control, bully, abuse, and steal from others for centuries. In more recent times, company owners and their hired managers have abused workers both emotionally and physically. Charles Dickens's novels of the Industrial Revolution era in England are now known to be accurate in their portrayals of the cruelty endured by the masses at the hands of those with money and power. In the early part of this century, Upton Sinclair wrote fiction that chronicled the hardships workers faced at the hands of American managers. It took new federal laws to ensure a minimum wage and to stop child labor, unfair work rules, unreasonably long working hours, and unsafe conditions in factories and mines. While not all companies, not all entrepreneurs, and not all managers were cruel, uncaring taskmasters, enough did fit this stereotype to require the government to intervene in private business.

Of course, the government itself has a less than spotless record among its leaders. Jokes equating politicians with criminals are common for a reason: we've been asked to "Read my lips" too many times, only to discover that promises have not been kept. Worse than this, we've watched in dismay as some of our elected leaders have been unmasked as successful con men who have been able to enrich themselves (or their supporters) because of their positions. We've been outraged to learn about their use of office to gain money, property, personal power, and even sex, when they were (or so we thought) supposed to be minding *our* business—looking out for our interests, safety, and betterment.

Whether our managers are officials that we have elected or the bosses at work, we don't trust them to look out for us. That lack of trust in the workplace was one of the factors contributing to the rise of organized labor. It still keeps workers in unions today.

In Government We Trust—Not

During a recent review of post-election poll results, Mark Mellman, CEO of Democratic polling firm Mellman-Lazarus-Lake, noted that the days when the American public held government officials in high esteem are long gone: "Trust in government has never been lower. In fact, in 1974, as we were about to impeach [then President Richard M. Nixon], more people trusted the government to do the right thing than trust the government to do the right thing today.

– AHA News, 12/5/94

Looking for Heroes in the Labor Union

Trust is needed in order for individuals to feel safe, and safety is an important motivator. In fact, psychologist Abraham Maslow's widely accepted theory claims that a sense of safety is one of the most basic human needs. Maslow's theory of motivation is that human behavior is driven by the desire to satisfy needs. His theory can be used by some to explain why employees join unions.[6]

According to Maslow, human needs are what motivate people. All needs are organized as a hierarchy, and only when the lower desires are met can higher wants motivate. In fact, only unsatisfied needs motivate.

Maslow's Hierarchy

Self-actualization (self-fulfillment)
Self-esteem (self-respect)
Social (belonging)
Safety (protection from danger and threat)
Physiological needs (food, clothing, shelter)

This is a simplified version of Maslow's theory, but it helps explain one reason for union membership. Safety is a basic need, and if workers feel that their job is not secure or their working conditions are unsafe, they're motivated to find a way to make these more secure. Unions can also serve

---

[6] Maslow, Abraham: A theory of human motivation, *Psychological Review*, Vol. 50, 1943, p. 380.

as organizations where social needs can be met, as in a fraternity or sorority.

Unions are seen by many as agencies of protection against discrimination, unfair treatment, arbitrary behavior, and even job loss at the hands of managers. The union official is seen as a hero who is needed to negotiate for better wages, benefits, and working conditions. When workers feel the need for this kind of protection, there is an implied lack of trust.

If unionization indicates a lack of trust between workers and managers, and Americans do not as a whole trust that today's business leaders can bring us out of the chaos and "slush," why don't 100 percent of all employees belong to unions? A variety of reasons exist, of course, reasons as complex as individuals and our society. But one explanation that must be considered as having some validity is this: unions themselves are not universally trusted. After all, union leaders are often represented in fiction and the media as being corrupt and self-serving. Major union officials are seen as well-paid bureaucrats themselves. In 1993, the executive board of Teamsters Local 705 in Chicago was removed from office because the union's independent review board found that they had engaged in a "pattern of financial malpractice." Their perks included $38,000 Lincoln Town Cars paid for by union dues. Since then, some executive board members have even been convicted of criminal activity. Reports of cheating union leaders, such as the former president of the Boeing Company's International Association of Machinists and Aerospace Workers (convicted in 1993 of embezzling union funds), add to the public mind's unflattering picture of labor leaders.[7]

One Union's Shame:
A Brief History of Corrupt Teamsters Leadership

Dave Beck	Union leader convicted for tax evasion and for selling union-owned Cadillacs for his own profit.
James Hoffa, Sr.	Union president convicted of mail fraud and jury tampering.
Frank Fitzsimmons	Union president who died while under federal investigation for using teamsters pension funds for loans to union officials' friends.
Roy Williams	Union president convicted in 1982 of attempting to bribe a United States senator.
Jackie Presser	Union president who was a defendant in federal racketeering case at time of his death.
Barry Feinstein	New York City Local 237 president forced to resign in 1993 when charged with embezzlement.

Some union members of today complain that union leaders are not admired any more than the company managers with whom they negotiate:

---

[7] Corporate Author, Former head of Boeing union sentenced for embezzling $6,700. Associated Press, September, 1993.

I never was a strong union supporter, but the final straw for me was when the big guy from back East was sent out to negotiate our contract . . . and he arrived at the hospital in a limousine.

– S. H., RN

I guess it's good to be in a union. I'd be afraid not to. I mean, the union gets us our money and all . . . but I know he [the union leader] doesn't really care about us. He just wants our dues so he can keep his job.

– R. T., clerk

Hey, union bosses are just as bad as other bosses. Why do you think they're called bosses?

– L. T., secretary

Some people who have been promoted into management positions haven't belonged there. That is, their abilities as leaders were not equal to the needs of their companies. Some politicians have been elected into positions where they have used their offices for personal gain. Some union officials have done the same thing. Does this mean that no manager is competent? That no politician is honest? That no union official really cares about the well-being of the workers she represents? Of course not! But if the movies, literature, television shows, and newspaper coverage of our times are representative of how Americans think, our society may truly believe that "boss" is synonymous with "bad person," whether that boss is our employer, a union leader, or an elected official.

All around us we're seeing, feeling, and living change. As previously mentioned, there's no time to refreeze. So here we are in the slush, looking for leaders to help us make it through the chaos, largely seeing our formal managers as objects of contempt, ridicule, or fear . . .

It's colder than a boss's heart.

> – Ron Macke, mailman, commenting
> on record low temperatures

The consensus is that our business executives are enriching themselves beyond any kind of acceptable level while impoverishing America.

> – James Patterson and Peter Kim,
> THE DAY AMERICA TOLD THE TRUTH

There is a bias in the public mind that executives are self-centered, egotistical individuals. They . . . are perceived as economic entities concerned primarily with gaining material advantage for themselves.

> – Rabendia Kanungo and Joy Conger,
> APPRECIATIVE MANAGEMENT AND LEADERSHIP, 1990

Nice guys can make bad bosses. . . .

> – Alan Loy McGinnis,
> BRINGING OUT THE BEST IN PEOPLE, 1985

Bosses more frequently than not disregard or don't see norms and rely on the exercise of unilateral power to compel shifts in behavior. . . .

> – Robert Blake and Jane Mouton,
> PRODUCTIVITY: THE HUMAN SIDE, 1982

Most people do not run across the "ogre boss" in their careers, but there are enough abrasive supervisors and managers to keep the threat of their presence abundant.

– Kathleen Ryan and Danile Ooestreude,
DRIVING FEAR OUT OF THE WORKPLACE, 1991

Most people in management are not aware that they are imprisoned by current practices of management . . . that these management practices are the cause of American corporate decline.

– W. Edwards Deming in
THE CHICAGO TRIBUNE, 12/29/91

I listen sometimes to the Sounds of the Workplace . . . the way the restaurant manager talks to the waiter, the way the foreman talks to the clerk. It isn't always easy on the ear. There is no right to be treated respectfully. No law against being humiliated. There is no equality of politeness between boss and bossed.

– Ellen Goodman, THE BOSTON GLOBE, 11/14/93

There are many people in high-level management whose cognitive capacity . . . is simply not adequate to grasp all the data with which they now must deal.

– Harry Levinson, the Academy of Management
publication THE EXECUTIVE, 1988

Bosses stand out either for their ineptitude in people management or their overall ineptitude in just about everything they touch or rub up against.

– Jon Hahn, The SEATTLE POST
INTELLIGENCER, 10/14/95

At the beginning of my career, I thought it would
be wonderful to be a college president some day.
But now I feel almost insulted when someone
approaches me with such a prospect. Do they
think I have NO principles and no backbone?

– Thomas Sowell, The Hoover Institute

Everybody's afraid of the Big Bad Boss . . .
Madison Avenue is increasingly portraying the
office as hell on earth, populated by screaming
bosses who relentlessly pile the work on their
suffering employees.

– THE WALL STREET JOURNAL, 1/12/94

Readers of the comic strip "Dilbert" are familiar
with bad bosses, the ones who micromanage,
terrorize staff, humiliate subordinates. They're
bosses from Hell and they're an increasingly
popular subject for organizational psychologists.

– Vanessa Ho, THE SEATTLE POST
INTELLIGENCER, 10/16/95

Being well acquainted with your boss . . . you
probably can accept that we descended from
apes.

– David Stip, "The Way We Were,"
THE WALL STREET JOURNAL, 5/24/95

Idiots promoted into management is the #1
frustration in the workplace.

– Scott Adams, DILBERT SURVEY, 1995

Leadership Yesterday and Today

Have Americans always seen their formal leaders and managers in a less than favorable light? Some authors have suggested that Americans had respect and trust for their political leaders until the assassination of John Kennedy. Their contention is that the President's death in Dallas, November 22, 1963, was the start of society's insecurity. Others blame the Viet Nam War and its coverage by the media as ushering in an age of cynicism, which has spread to include a distrust of any authority figure. Perhaps it's true that the general population has less faith in leaders today, but history is marked with examples of leaders who have not been considered heroes by those they led:

> *Workers have nothing to lose but their chains.*
>
> — COMMUNIST MANIFESTO of Karl Marx
> and Friedrich Engels, 1848

> *Mr. Roosevelt is the only man we ever had in the White House who would understand that my boss is a son-of-a-bitch.*
>
> — A 1936 working man, quoted by
> Thomas Baily in VOICES OF AMERICA

> *Carnegie had amassed a huge personal fortune, even though he was well aware that many of his own steel workers were not well paid. But he made no apology for the inequality, and in fact defended it as survival of the fittest.*
>
> — G. Cavenaugh, AMERICAN BUSINESS
> VALUES IN TRANSITION, 1976

Her protagonist was a young woman who faced exploitation and degrading factory discipline from bosses in a male-oriented society.

   – M. V. Tyler, A Book Without a Title, 1855

Magnates of the late 1800s came to be known as 'tycoons, moguls, or robber barons' . . . they often engaged in methods that are unethical by any high standard.

   – N. Foerster and Robert Falk, American Poetry and Prose, 1960

Early entrepreneurs were "tyrannical, hard, sometimes cruel."

   – Paul Mantoux, The Industrial Revolution in the 18th Century, 1928

John D. Rockefeller was one of the most hated men of his day — a ruthless financier who amassed incredible wealth by undercutting and eliminating competitors.

   – William Manchester, A Rockefeller Family Portrait, 1958

The working class and the employing class have nothing in common.

   – The Constitution of the Industrial Workers of the World, 1905

If managers down through history were not held in high esteem by their employees, neither were the employees regarded well by their leaders:

*In society, men of command positions are fathers
and lesser folks are children.*

> – Henry Wood, NATURAL LAW IN
> THE BUSINESS WORLD, 1887

*Workers are whiskey-bloated and heavy-brained
Irish, Dutch, and Blacks with souls half asleep.*

> – Rebecca Harding Davis,
> MARGRET HOWTH, 1862

*What a sorry set of ignoramuses they must be . . .
in combining together to prevent other men from
working for low wages because, forsooth, they are
discontented with them.*

> – Henry May, PROTESTANT CHURCHES
> AND INDUSTRIAL AMERICA, quoting
> the CHRISTIAN UNION of 1877

*If a person can get sufficient income in four days to
support himself for seven days he will keep holiday
the other three; that is, he will live in riot and de-
bauchery.*

> – J. Powess, A VIEW OF REAL GRIEVANCES (1771),
> quoted in A. Brigg's HOW THEY LIVED, 1969

*The rights and interests of the laboring man will be
protected and cared for . . . by the Christian men to
whom God in His infinite wisdom has given control
of the property interests of the country . . .*

> – from a 1903 letter written by the president of the
> Philadelphia and Reading Railroad, as documented
> in Herbert Harris's AMERICAN LABOR, 1939

The one is master and depends on profits. The other is servant and depends on salary.

– Andrew Carnegie on the division
between managers and employees

Bosses Today—Who Are They?

When we talk about bosses in American organizations, we're speaking largely of white males. In the 38,059 United States companies that reported to the U.S. Equal Opportunities Commission in 1992, men held two-thirds of the managerial jobs. Men occupy three-fourths of the "officials and managers" category in the two hundred biggest companies, and make up 95 percent of executives at the vice presidential level.[8]

A typical CEO is fifty-six years old, male, white, and Protestant. According to a 1993 study of a thousand large American companies, the typical CEO has been in the top job an average of 8.5 years and at his company twenty-one years. He came up through the ranks. He is most likely to come from the Northeast or Midwest. He is well-educated. In fact, 90 percent of the CEOs in these large companies have college degrees and more than half have graduate education (with the MBA degree most prevalent). Two percent never went to college. Seven percent didn't graduate with a degree.[9]

---

[8] Sharpe, R.: "The waiting game; women make strides but men stay firmly in top company jobs." Wall Street Journal, March 29, 1994.

[9] Bhargava, S. and Jesperson, F.: "Portrait of a CEO", *Business Week,* October 11, 1993.

What about leaders in small companies? Out of two hundred small company leaders in 1993, five CEOs were over age seventy, five were under forty, and the rest fell into the middle-aged years. The majority were college-educated, many with graduate education (20 percent had MBAs, but there were other masters degrees, as well as doctorate level degrees in the group).

Who Should the Bosses Be?

The appropriate background of managers has been the subject of long-standing debate. At issue has been the efficacy of hiring "professional" managers who are generalists versus promoting workers into management positions. Management theorists have been divided in their opinions. Some believe that a good manager can manage anything and does not need to have firsthand experience as a technician, professional, or front-line worker in the type of department or company managed. Others hold that the best managers have a background that includes expertise in the kind of work being managed.

> In the 1960s, the CEO thought he could manage anything. The substance of business wasn't important. This was a mind set that was a disaster, partly because it cut the CEO off from reality. In the 1970s, many chiefs, ill-informed about the business, ignored the threat of foreign competition.
>
> – Alfred D. Chandler, Jr., corporate historian,
> THE WALL STREET JOURNAL, 9/11/97

One school of thought is that different levels of management need different ratios of technical, conceptual, and interpersonal skills. Technical skills are abilities needed to perform specific tasks. Interpersonal skills refer to ability and judgment in working with people. Conceptual skills are defined as understanding a complex organization and an individual's place within it. Supervisors at the lower levels need considerable technical skill, while top managers concentrate on the conceptual side of leadership. All levels need interpersonal skills.

> *People who are smart in leadership should be in charge and people who are smart about technical things should be subordinates. But you often get the situation of people being promoted just because they weren't smart enough to be subordinates.*
>
> – Scott Adams, creator of the comic strip "Dilbert"

Research studies have shown that some groups resist and are insubordinate when their managers don't have expert knowledge of the group's work tasks. Other research has shown that the dual role of the professional/technician and manager has caused problems in executive-suite decision making. Insufficient weight is assigned to the financial implications of decisions by managers who come from professional/technical backgrounds. These managers find themselves motivated by dual, often conflicting standards: those of their organization and those of their professional colleagues. The result is reduced organizational effectiveness.

Experts disagree about appropriate management background. Beyond the question of whether the best bosses come from within the work force or start their careers as managers for workers whose jobs they have never performed, is the issue of how workers themselves feel about where their managers come from. Frequently, how bosses are perceived centers around trust and whether or not the managers both understand and care about the work their employees perform. To the workers in the organization, it is easier to believe that someone who's been on the front lines cares about what happens there:

> I get so sick of her telling us what to do. She [the department head] gives us impossible tasks because she's never done this kind of work. How can she possibly understand what we're going through?
>
> – A records file clerk

> I may not always agree with what the boss does. But, you know, it makes it easier to swallow some of her decisions because she always gives us a rationale, and her explanations make it clear she knows about our jobs—she's done them herself.
>
> – A union shop steward

> I don't care if the manager's ever done my job, I just care that if he hasn't done it, he doesn't interfere with me doing it. I'm the expert and he should keep his nose out of stuff he doesn't know anything about.
>
> – A factory worker

*We tried this experiment where the superinten-
dent of the school district was a business person
with no background in education. It failed miser-
ably. He just couldn't understand how difficult it is
for teachers in the classroom. He couldn't see the
challenges faced by a principal trying to run an
individual school.*

— A school administrator

*I spend most of my time trying to explain to the
male vice presidents how the hospital runs at the
patient-care level. Since they started their careers at
the assistant administrator level, they have no idea
about the complexities of the work done by nurses
and ancillary staff members . . . even after decades
in the hospital field.*

— A vice president for hospital nursing services

What about women and minorities as bosses? Historically
excluded from leadership roles, women have not reached
executive positions in large numbers. Stereotypes suggest
that females lack a commitment to their careers and that
they are undependable and too emotional. Their status is
lower in our society than that of men, and various research
studies have indicated that women's promotions in management are hindered by discrimination from male admini-
strators who have the power to select who will "move up the
ladder." The "glass ceiling" is seen as preventing capable
women from attaining leadership positions.

In a management system based on paternalism, it makes
sense that women have not been seen as appropriate top

managers. After all, bosses have been stereotyped too. Historically we've believed the effective manager is masculine, as well as competent and tough. He must take charge, make decisions, and provide discipline to the company. Women have been seen as too warm, too emotional to provide the leadership needed in business.

We've believed that the top bosses must be males. That is, we've believed it until recently. Now management writers ranging from feminists to male management theorists are suggesting that a new leadership style will be needed for the future. And they're describing that style as something we've always thought of as *feminine*.

> *Women's' childhood socialization is more in step with today's successful corporate cultures: managers need to be nurturers, coaches, need to be able to mediate disputes, compromise, teach, and so on.*
>
> – Diane Cohen, Canadian newswoman, in WOMEN IN MANAGEMENT, August/September 1993

> *The new executives, I project, will be more sensitive and more aware of their own feelings.*
>
> – Harry Levinson of the Levinson Institute, in the Academy of Management publication THE EXECUTIVE, 1988, Vol. II, No. 2

> *The womanly approach to leadership may be the style of the future.*
>
> – Judith Rosener, University of California professor, quoted by Shirley Sharzer of the Soulham Newspaper Group

Leadership experts are calling for changes in management and leadership styles; the qualities they are advocating are especially congruent with the behaviors most women exhibit because of the way women are socialized in our culture.

– Dr. Beverly A. Forbes, consultant, Renton, Washington

We suggest we look to women to get us out of our generally acknowledged crisis of leadership. Their talents and moral qualities are underused. Women lie less, are more responsible, and are far more honest at work.

– James Patterson and Peter Kim,
THE DAY AMERICA TOLD THE TRUTH

Intellectually, people may agree that it's time we had more women as top leaders. But in actuality, although the number of women managers increased 14 percent from 1981 to 1991, the increase in women at the senior executive level was only 2 percent. This increase in female middle managers has not automatically changed the type of leadership that prevails in organizations. Women bosses have often been promoted not because of their innate feminine way of leading, but because they learned to emulate the masculine, detached, unemotional leadership styles of their own bosses. Now, however, the message is going out to male and female managers alike that the future is going to require a different, more caring (let's call it loving) style *and it may be easier for women to adopt this way of leading.*

Minority leaders have had their own glass ceilings to contend with. Promotion into management positions has societal, traditional, and cultural implications that are only magnified for them. Some minority managers may have faced prejudice that has kept them from climbing corporate ladders. Some others may have been promoted to a certain level (not the very top), not because of their leadership ability, but because of affirmative action programs. In other words, their minority status may cause these bosses to be held to either more stringent or less demanding standards than others. In this respect, women and male minorities have similar stereotypes and challenges to overcome.

Increasing evidence shows that a new, multicultural work force is going to be a major aspect of business in the future. It makes intuitive sense that leaders from varied cultural backgrounds will have an easier time adapting to the managing of this work force.

Another question about leaders concerns their education. Do managers need formal education? If so, what should it be, and should the requirements differ from industry to industry? There are managers with no college degree, particularly among small businesses. In larger industries, all types of educational backgrounds can be found. The Master's in Business Administration has become common for would-be and current managers in every industry because the general population seems to see the MBA as a ticket into better jobs.

In business schools, students learn finance, accounting, production, marketing, applied math, applied economics, and varying amounts of behavioral sciences. Some business experts feel that a business degree is being earned by too many people; they urge businesses to hire managers with liberal arts degrees in recognition of a need for "people skills" such as communication and interpersonal relations. What do the people being managed think their bosses' education should be? Most aren't concerned with college degrees! They are interested in the personal characteristics of the people in charge, not their education.

In multiple management seminars conducted by the author for current and would-be supervisors, more than five hundred attendees were asked to think of the best and the worst boss they had ever had, and then to list the characteristics of those bosses. The lists compiled at each seminar were remarkable for their consistency from group to group (see summary on the next page). Formal education degrees weren't listed even once.

Of course, managers aren't usually hired by their employees. They're hired by boards of directors or upper management. What those who do the hiring are looking for isn't necessarily what is wanted by those who are to be managed. The classical goal for management of a firm is to "increase the value" of the firm for its owners. In many cases today, that means increasing the value of the stockholders' investments and/or making a profit. It's supposedly understood that "good management" will ensure these things. And the proof of "good management" can be found on the balance sheet or company's annual report, not in whether the employees rate their managers as good or bad.

And yet, could it be that the balance sheet would look better if workers and managers liked and respected each other? Could our companies' and our country's economic future be brighter if we really believed that our bosses, our leaders, cared about us, our products, and our companies?

What progress might we be able to make together, if we put our organizations in the hands of loving leaders, regardless of their education or background?

The Best Boss	The Worst Boss
Fair	Unfair
Consistent	Inconsistent
Competent	Incompetent
A problem solver	Wishy-washy
A listener	Overly opinionated
Flexible	Inflexible
Trustworthy	A backstabber
Straightforward	A liar
Knowledgeable	Uninformed
A good communicator	A poor communicator
Action-oriented	Risk-averse
Honest	Dishonest
Respectful	Demeaning
Admirable and inspirational	Unethical
A teacher and mentor	A hoarder of information
Future oriented	Tradition-bound
Open	Secretive
Courteous	Rude
Inclusive	Divisive
Modest	Takes credit for others' work
Kind	Mean-spirited
Generous with praise	Never praises others
Patient	Demanding

Manager or Leader: Who's the Boss?

It's popular today to contrast "leaders" with "managers" because current thought is that leadership doesn't equal management. While classical management includes planning, controlling, directing, and evaluating, leaders guide, mentor, inspire, and develop as they lead people. Management is defined as a discipline that can be learned in how-to classes: how to interview, how to delegate, how to write a budget, how to do a flow chart, how to evaluate people and products.

Leadership is seen as more of an art, not learned in formal classes but practiced by influential managers and nonmanagers alike.

> Leadership is a concept of owing certain things to the institution. . . . To be a leader means, especially, having the opportunity to make a meaningful difference in the lives of those who permit leaders to lead.
>
> – Max DePree, LEADERSHIP IS AN ART

> Traditional management systems have been devised to achieve control and maintain direction. True leadership draws its followers along by developing rather than directing.
>
> – Marlys E. Nuis and Ruth T. Kengelar,
> LEADERSHIP IN TRANSITION

> With changes in the roles of the leaders in team organizations, "controllers," "planners," and "inspectors" are replaced with "coaches," "facilitators," and "supporters."
>
> – Richard Wellins, William Byham, and
> Jeanne Wilson, EMPOWERED TEAMS

A leader knows what's best to do; a manager merely knows how best to do it.

— Ken Adelman,
Tribune Media Services

Both the how-to skills of management and the inspirational skills of leadership are needed for the success of an organization, but it's leadership that people ask for. When have you heard someone say, "What we need in this company (or country) is management!" What you have probably heard is, "What we need in this country is leadership!" And the leaders most likely to be followed are those in whom followers see (no matter what they call it) the evidence of love.

Maternalistic Management: The Evidence of Love

To speak of loving leaders may seem to some to imply only that the best leaders are those who are kind, considerate, and empathic. While these are traits all of us may say we desire in our managers, they don't fully describe a loving leader. The truly loving leader can be recognized as much by what she or he *is not* as by what she or he *is*. To reiterate what was learned from five hundred seminar attendees:

A Loving Leader *Is Not* . . .

self-centered	sadistic	cold
self-important	self-aggrandizing	unethical
a bigot	routinely inconsiderate	uninterested
cruel	routinely rude	dishonest

Nor Is She or He . . .

self-effacing	self-sacrificing	"soft"
a martyr	wishy-washy	a wimp
masochistic	unrealistic about people	a doormat
a pushover	always politically correct	risk-averse

Nor Is She or He Necessarily . . .

humble	universally liked	popular

A loving leader cares for the people who work with her, but she also loves her organization, its products, its customers, and herself. She must make decisions based on concern for all the players in the complex world of work. Rather than concentrating totally on the classical management job of maximizing benefits for stockholders, she understands that the best leaders work to maximize benefits for all the stakeholders. And stakeholders are everyone whose life is affected by the success (or failure) of the organization—including stockholders.

Managers capable of this type of leadership are the true "big picture" people. They're not just the so-called big picture executives who are able to see how their companies fit into their industry and the world economy, but leaders who can see how all the pieces, both large and small, fit together. They are able to juggle the demands of various stakeholders, and to understand that these demands may not always appear complementary. They are visionaries who are able to see beyond the here and now, who can forego the "quick wins" of today for the benefits of a prosperous, long-term future.

Because they're loving, they want that prosperity for everyone involved.

You might think that this description of loving leadership equals an endorsement of the practices of paternalism. It doesn't. Paternalism is a way of leading or governing people by providing for their needs *without giving them responsibility.* Paternalism is a sort of "Father (or Mother) knows best" philosophy, so if you just do what Pater (the leader) says, you will be provided for in the manner that is best for you. A loving organization is one in which maternalism is practiced, one in which leaders demonstrate their caring by providing a work environment where every single worker can grow and develop to his or her full potential. Maternalism means valuing others by providing education and opportunity. It means respect for others, because respected people are given responsibility. Just as a mother robin teaches her young to fly so that they can someday fend for themselves, the maternalistic leader (male or female) provides followers with opportunities for learning and growth, so that someday they won't need him or her.

Management or Manipulation?

New management theories with new names have been widely preached and widely accepted over the years. People with even minimal management education are aware of Maslow's Hierarchy, Theories Y and X, "Japanese" management, Theory Z, MBO (Management by Objective), situational management, and the quality management terms, CQI and TQM (Continuous Quality Improvement and Total Quality Management). Organizations spend hundreds of thousands—

even millions—of dollars, hiring consultants and educators to train their managers in management theory and skills. Yet we still see poor management. Within our organizations, when one theory doesn't work, we abandon it and move on to something else. We proclaim, "We tried TQM and it doesn't work!" We try something else, and it doesn't "work" either! Why is this? Each of these management theories may very well be the right thing to do. The problem is that "the right thing" becomes "not right" when it's not done for the right reasons.

Class after class and seminar after seminar teaches this or that way to manage people. Most of what is presented is appealing because intuitively it seems to be correct. The problem is that what is taught to managers as good management is only a disguised form of manipulation.

Why is it manipulation? Because of the *reasons* it's being espoused:

1. If you practice this type of management, you'll be able to compete and win over the competition.

2. If you practice this type of management, you'll have contented employees and win over the unions.

3. If you practice this type of management, productivity will be increased.

4. If you practice this type of management, profits will be increased.

5. If you practice this type of management, costs will be decreased.

Are competitiveness, good employee relations, high productivity, high profits, and low costs unimportant? Of course not! All are valid—in fact, essential—business goals. However, they are surface-level goals which need to be anchored in a deeper, more fundamental concern for the customers, employees, company, and managers. The reason that sound management theory fails when it is put into practice is because in day-to-day business this loving concern is either absent or suppressed. Nor is it expressed in management classes or "leadership" training.

Most management amounts to manipulation for the manager's own advantage. In the long run, it is seen for what it is, and it falls short of its promise. Loving leadership, or maternalism, is the missing ingredient that could make management work for the good of all stakeholders.

The History, Present, and Future of Management Theory

It is hard to recognize when the past ends and the future begins, but we are living on such a hinge of history.

– V. Clayton Sherman, CREATING THE
NEW AMERICAN HOSPITAL

Throughout human history there has been some sort of management, but the first recognized management book wasn't printed until 1832. It was written by James Montgomery in Glasgow, Scotland.[1] Writing for the cotton industry, Montgomery talked about quality, quantity, and keeping costs down. He also emphasized the need for preventing faults rather than finding and correcting them after they occur (the first inklings of TQM and CQI!).

---

[1] Montgomery, James: The Carding and Spinning Masters' Assistant; or The Theory and Practice of Cotton Spinning. Glasgow: J. Neven, Jr., 1832.

Historical Thinking

After Montgomery, management theorists proliferated. They wrote books, lectured, experimented, and argued with each other. Some of them took management positions so they could practice what they preached. Several of these early authors still influence what managers are taught today. In the late 1700s and early 1800s, people like Charles Babbage and Daniel McCallum espoused strong ideas about how work should be accomplished. They saw a need for a division of labor (into skilled, semi-skilled, and unskilled workers) and for specialization, or the division of responsibilities among laborers. They believed in the importance of rigid discipline, the formal organization chart, and strict communication lines.

The late 1800s and early 1900s were the years of "Scientific Management." That generation of management thinkers believed that the best way to do any worker's job should be determined scientifically: jobs could be broken down into tasks, studied, and then put back together for performance with the utmost efficiency. Time and motion studies came out of this era, as well as ideas about the need to match people's abilities to their jobs. Frederick Taylor was one theorist who felt that job standards should be set by management for all workers, while another consultant, Frank Gilbreth, determined that labor should take part in setting their own standards. Others began to realize that psychology, sociology, and even anthropology have something to do with human behavior at work. Management expert Lillian Gilbreth felt that not only is there a psychology involved in management, but management can and should help develop each individual worker to reach his highest potential.

Ideas about the social element of work followed the early scientific managers. Elton Mayo was associated with experiments that showed that there is a relationship between working conditions and human performance at work. Mary Parker Follett felt that conflict between managers and workers can be reduced if they understand and work toward goals that benefit both. She also introduced the interesting thought that workers work "with" a manager, not "under" a boss.

A Few Thoughts From Early Management Theorists

Charles Babbage (1792-1871):

There should be a division of labor. Profit sharing with workers could increase productivity.

Daniel McCallum (1815-1878):

There should be a formal organization chart, rigid discipline, and rigid communication lines.

Henri Fayol (1841-1925):

Good management is essential for good organizational performance. Management must be taught, based on management theory.

Henry Lawrence Gantt (1861-1919):

Labor and management have mutual interests. Education for the worker must include how to be industrious and cooperate as well as how to do the job.

Frederick Taylor (1856-1915):

> There is a proper way to design each job. There is
> a scientific way to perform each task. Standards are
> best set by management.

Frank Gilbreth (1868-1924):

> You can find the "best" way to perform tasks
> through time and motion studies. It's best to enlist
> the cooperation of labor in setting their standards.

Mary Parker Follett (1868-1933):

> Conflict between management and workers can be
> reduced by an integration of interests. Leadership
> should be based on reciprocal influence, not power.

Lillian M. Gilbreth (1878-1972):

> There is a definite managerial psychology. Manage-
> ment can help develop each individual to his fullest
> potential.

Elton Mayo (1880-1949):

> There is a relationship between working conditions
> and human performance at work.

Luther Gulick (1897-1993):

> The functions of an executive are to plan, organize,
> staff, direct, coordinate, report, and budget.

Rensis Likert (1903-1981):

> Leading human resources is the most important
> of all a manager's tasks.

Managers who have received formal education in the past few decades have heard all of these theories. They're also familiar with currently popular ideas. Today, the theories that managers either embrace with a passion or are being force-fed revolve around issues of quality. Challenged by competition from abroad, American companies have fallen behind in efficiency and productivity. In order to compete, we feel the need to increase productivity and improve quality, hence the emphasis on CQI (Continuous Quality Improvement) and TQM (Total Quality Management). While the intellectuals at the universities argue fine points of theory (sometimes quite vehemently), management teams grasp at the latest ideas, anxious to try something, *anything,* that's new. There really isn't anything totally new. As is indicated by the brief review of managerial history chronicled above, today's thoughts are yesterday's thoughts, recombined or repackaged! That doesn't make them any less valid. In fact, maybe they have become more valid because so many of the ideas, whether titled "Montgomery's Cotton Quality Theory," "TQM," or "CQI," have survived over time and still intuitively appeal to those of us who earn our living by working as managers.

Okay, so management theory has evolved and is still evolving. What does that mean for those of us who work in organizations today, and plan to be working in them (whatever their form) tomorrow? A number of futurists and management theorists are writing and speaking about leadership and about what we're going to need to see in our leaders as we approach a new century. Some base their thoughts on research, while others serve up ideas that capture our collective imaginations because they seem so much like common sense. Based on our own individual experiences as —or with—bosses, on the trauma of slipping through slush, and on the general state of the world, each of us has formed our own theories on management. We don't usually think of our opinions as theories, and we probably don't even realize we believe them until they're articulated by someone else. Yet what we do, as leaders or followers, is based on our personal beliefs about people, society, values, and what has worked for us.

What Is Your Personal Theory of Management?

Management is the allocation and direction of limited resources—time, talent, and money—in the completion of tasks and organizational objectives.

– Rick D., MBA student

My personal theory for management and leadership is "Understand your personal values." Once you recognize those guiding values, hard decisions become less difficult. Colleagues and staff come to know and understand your management ways as you are consistent in practice. The best value for me: Live the behaviors you wish to develop in others.

– Marla B., department head

Compensate your people for outstanding effort. Credit should be given for the job done well, and not given when not earned.

– Jack E., small business owner

The best management seeks out and develops various talents, abilities, and potential in their staff, and fosters individual or organizational growth. The worst management turns human beings into inhabitants of a sea of mediocrity.

— Cris D., administrative assistant

I'm a benevolent dictator — I get ideas and advice from others but I make the final decision. I'm the one responsible.

— Bill S., airline captain

In spite of having our own theories, we are continually looking for new ideas, new ways to manage. Management seminars are conducted weekly all over the nation. Consultants in every industry are available to instruct leaders in the nuts and bolts of managing people. While the "scientists" of management, the professors studying and teaching theory, are busy measuring, comparing, and debating (and criticizing other people's studies, measurements, and theories), practicing managers want practical, surefire answers about doing their jobs. We're willing to pay to hear what "experts" have to say.

What are they telling us these days? Although different delivery styles and "tools" are offered by the various individuals and firms, the messages going out are much the same:

1. It is time for the empowerment of our workers (and our customers).

2. Managers need to be concerned with individual dignity and worth.

3. Great leaders bring out the best in others.

4. People-centered management is the way to go.

5. Autonomy, self-direction, self-governance, and decentralized control are part of the new litany for leadership.

6. Transformational leadership will change the workplace forever, as we make "managers" into "coordinators," "employees" into "associates," and work into pleasure.

7. In other words, Lillian Gilbreth and Mary Parker Follett were on to something!

The implications of all this? We haven't managed correctly in the past. The inference? If we change our styles and our vocabulary we will succeed in improving our productivity and competitiveness in the world economy. The missing ingredient? True concern for our co-workers, colleagues, companies, and customers. But calling employees "associates" (as some experts advise) does not automatically improve our relationships. If the sole motive for all of these prescribed transformations into a "people-centered organization" is still profit, the changes in the organization still come down to simple manipulation.

Manipulation will lead to failure, partly because people eventually see through it and partly because manipulators are usually looking for quick fixes. We in business buy, and "buy into" (for short increments of time), management products with specific prescriptions to follow and specific tools to use, because that's easier than using our own creativity. We've tried management by objectives, re-engineering, change management, horizontal and vertical integration, core competencies, learning organizations, overhead value analysis, service quality, strategic planning, time-based management, total quality management, and benchmarking. Now we're being told that we're on the brink of a new leadership era, in which organization managers will become less "controllers" and more "coordinators," less "bosses" and more "coaches." The ideas are *right*, but still missing the ingredient that will make it all work: maternalism.

Today's Thinking

Just as mothering is not really the opposite of fathering (good parenting shares commonalties, whatever the gender of the parent), maternalism is not the opposite of paternalism. But it's not the same thing, either.

Paternalism is the ancient set of behaviors practiced throughout civilization by tribes, churches, and countries and based on the idea that the leader is the father of the group. Leaders are responsible for the welfare of everyone in the organization. Some earlier American businesses carried this philosophy to the point where it was felt that they must provide meals, housing, education, and recreation for their company "families." One example was the textile manufacturers of the 1800s who tried to employ only young females, house them in company boarding houses, and monitor their moral conduct. Early nursing schools did the same with their nurse trainees, and there are numerous other such examples.

In 1897, the National Cash Register Company's managers included a "welfare director" whose job was to improve the workers' lives at work and at home. Joseph Bancroft and Sons, H.H. Heinz, and Westinghouse Electric were a few of the other companies that adopted a model whereby managers were specifically assigned to look after the nutritional, recreational, educational, and interpersonal needs of employees.

On the surface, this concern for employees is laudable, but its Achilles' heel is that the entire premise underlying paternalism is that the company (or the company's leader) knows what is best for everyone in the company. In other words, managers must be responsible for those they manage because workers are like children, unable to lead themselves. They will never grow to maturity because, if they did, they would then be managers! Mature, adult managers must make decisions for the immature working population. The "benevolent dictator" represents the practical paternalistic management style.

Strong traces of paternalism still abide in organizations today. Leaders who would be horrified to be labeled "paternalistic" still base their practices on old management-always-knows-best beliefs. And paternalism, like so many human practices, proves to be a self-fulfilling prophecy. When children are not given authority or responsibility, most do not mature into responsible adults. When first-line workers are not given authority or responsibility, many are unprepared for it and unable to cope with it when it *is* "given" to them.

"Maturity" and "immaturity" are terms used in describing the development of children into fully grown adults. In the workplace, the same words can be used in describing the development of workers, as regards their skills, education, interpersonal relationships, and willingness and ability to take

> *You've got all kinds of people who make a living and support themselves but who psychologically are not grown up. We have a culture of functional immaturity.*
>
> – Leon Kass, Professor of Social Thought, University of Chicago

responsibility, solve problems, and lead themselves and/or others. Organizational maturity does not necessarily correlate with age or job seniority. It is startling to realize how much adults can resemble children. We have some of the same ways of reacting to problems and stress, and many of the same self-esteem needs.

Many would find it offensive to compare companies (or churches or nations) to parents of children, or to speak of "adult" managers and "childlike" employees. Offensive or not, paternalism has set us up as a society where many working people are treated like children and many have not matured in their workplace roles. A spin-off of paternalism is a type of management that nursing leader Marie Manthey, RN, calls "Mama Management."[2] She says that managers who practice this method repeatedly move in to take over problems and solve them for staff members, thereby perpetuating juvenile behaviors and reinforcing the idea that the staff members are not capable of managing their own problems.

---

[2] Manthey, Marie: From 'mamma management' to team spirit. *Nursing Management*, January, 1990, page 20-21.

Paternalism and Mama Management are the antithesis of current leadership thought! They simply don't jibe with autonomy, self-direction, self-governance, and decentralized control. Today's slushy and tomorrow's even slushier world of change does call for leaders who can let go of control and empower their working colleagues, but unless those leaders recognize and encourage the maturity of the work force, their enlightened leadership is doomed to fail. In that event, a few years from now we'll be in another cycle of management thought, with new consultants telling us what to do (or the same ones singing different tunes), because we bought into a certain theory, wanted to be "transformational," empowered the workers, and then failed to sustain increased productivity or to improve the bottom line for the long term. Aspects of paternalism got us into this mess, Ollie. It will take maternalism to get us out.

> *The number-one thing employees say they want from a manager is: Make me feel good about myself and my work.*
>
> – Walter S. Brown, management consultant

> *One of the most important aspects of being a leader is to mend broken spirits and to develop a supportive work atmosphere that encourages worker involvement and fosters employee growth.*
>
> – W. Bickham, author of LIBERATING THE HUMAN SPIRIT IN THE WORKPLACE

The Effects of Paternalism in Modern Business

Men need to be the CEOs;
women are only promoted
so far (the glass ceiling) . . .

because paternalism . . .
implies it takes a strong male parent
(father figure) to be in charge.

Information about the company's
or the department's plans, the
leader's rationale, or any problems
is management's business only and
shouldn't be shared with employees,
so information is shared on a "need-
to-know"—never a "nice-to-know"—
basis, and management determines
the need to know . . .

because paternalism . . .
implies that only the adult managers
can be trusted with information.
Employee children wouldn't understand anyway.

Managers pick one favored subordinate
to develop in a formal mentorship, and
fail to provide the same opportunities
for other subordinates . . .

because paternalism . . .
encourages a father figure to
develop "a son who is like me to take
over the family when I'm gone."

Employees who are "empowered"
to make decisions or to self-manage
refuse to take this responsibility,
saying, "Manager, that's your job"...

because paternalism . . .
has trained them to avoid taking
responsibility.

There is fear in the workplace . . .

because paternalism . . .
implies that the parent (boss) has
tremendous power over your life.
Strong, powerful fathers are
feared, even if they are admired.

Hiring discrimination against
certain groups of workers,
such as gay people, is a given . . .

because paternalism . . .
implies that the children's (the
employees') personal lives reflect
on the father (the boss or company).

The Meaning of Maternalism

Paternalism has been identified with fathering, maternalism with mothering. In human society, fathers have been the family leaders, responsible for guiding, deciding, and meting out discipline. Mothers have been the supporters, nurturers, and dispensers of love. Until very recent history, fathers were "Mr. Outside," providing for the material needs of the family while mothers were at home, raising the children. The way that children mature and "turn out" has most frequently been attributed to their mothers.

In nature, it is the mother's responsibility to teach and care for her offspring so that, when they mature enough to leave her, they will be able to care for themselves. The mother robin teaches fledglings to fly, just as the lioness teaches cubs to hunt. Maternalism, as practiced in work settings or politics, is based on the kind of care that, among most creatures, amounts to mothering. But this kind of care, when applied to human young, is now recognized as good parenting—whether it is given by the mother or the father.

Because we are not known as a society of excellent parents, to say that management is based on the same principles as parenting may evoke instant skepticism. "I sure wouldn't want *my* mom for a boss!" might be the reaction.

Why not? Would she be such a bad manager? To this, people might answer as follows:

"She's such a perfectionist—I'd never be good enough."

"You've heard of 'smother love.' Well, that's my mother. I'd never be able to do anything on my own."

"She's the reason I'm so messed up already. I don't want to be more messed up at work!"

"I couldn't deal with that whole guilt trip" (or with the nagging, favoritism, neglect, or whatever Mom's imperfection is).

Mothers, being human, are imperfect. Managers, being human, are also imperfect. But both parenting and management can be done very well when parents and leaders carry out their roles on the basis of knowledge and love. The knowledge ideally includes an understanding of psychology, human development, and human relations, together with the necessary technical skills. The love is a true concern for others. Maternalism, as a management theory, is based on the similarity of needs between children growing up to be mature adults and adults growing into mature members of the business community. The psychology, the human development, and the human-relations needs involved in both processes are remarkably similar.

Parenting	Managing
In troubled families, self-worth is low, communication is vague, and rules are rigid, nonhumane, and nonnegotiable. In nurturing families, self-worth is high, communication is direct, clear, specific, and honest, and rules are flexible, humane, and appropriate.	In dysfunctional companies, communication is vague and rules are rigid, nonhumane, and nonnegotiable. In nurturing companies, self-worth is high and communication is direct, clear, specific, and honest. There is consideration for others and creativity in problem solving. Rules are flexible, humane, and appropriate.

Parenting	Managing
"A question for your family: Does it feel good to live in your family? Do you feel that you live with friends, people you like and trust, and who like and trust you? Is it fun and exciting to be a member of your family? . . . Things just don't happen by themselves in a family. Some guidance is necessary." – Virginia Satir, courtesy of Avanta, The Virginia Satir Network	A question for your workplace: Does it feel good to work here? Do you feel that you work with friends, people you like and trust, and who like and trust you? Is it fun and exciting to work at your company? Successful companies realize that trans-formational, empowering organizations still need guidance from a leader or leaders.
"Skillful parenting hinges on letting go. The most effective parents let children make mis-takes, realizing that the most valuable lessons in life are learned through trial and error." – John Rosemond, psychologist	Skillful management hinges on letting go. The most effective managers allow employees to take risks for the sake of discovery, innovation, creativity, and growth.
"Powerlessness corrupts children." – John Holt, HOW CHILDREN LEARN	Powerlessness corrupts workers.

Parenting

"Families can be evaluated as functioning in a healthy manner by their: adaptations (use of family resources for problem solving during crisis), partnerships (shared decision making and nurturing of responsibility by family members), growth (maturation and self-fulfillment of family members), affection (love in the family), and resolve (commitment to devote time to and share wealth with family members). Measurement of these functions involves looking at how resources are shared, the degree of family member satisfaction, and how decisions are made and shared."

– G. Smilkstein,
THE FAMILY APGAR

"A parent may have certain protective responsibilities by virtue of her role, but at a deeper level there's also an equality." – Dr. Peter Senge

Managing

Workplaces can be evaluated for good function by the company's use of resources during stressful periods, by the workers' taking part in decision making, by the encouragement of worker responsibility and self-actualization, by the mutual support and affection of company members, and by the associates' commitment to sharing resources with one another.

Measurement of these functions involves looking at how resources are shared, the degree of associate satisfaction, and how company decisions are made and shared.

A leader may have certain management responsibilities by virtue of his or her role, but at a deeper level there is also an equality.

Parenting	Managing
"When you are a mother, you are never really alone in your thoughts. A mother always has to think twice, once for herself and once for her child." – Sophia Loren, actress	A leader has to think about everyone's good: the company's, the associates', and the customers', as well as his or her own good.
"Mothers develop skills that successful leaders need. They nurture their charges. They act as role models and help in setting and reaching goals. They negotiate and mediate." – Kelly Butt, Senior Vice President of Information Services, London Life	Successful leaders develop skills that mothers and fathers need. They nurture, act as role models, help in setting and reaching goals, and negotiate and mediate.

Just as excellent parents are models for children to observe and learn from, excellent leaders serve as models for others. Excellent parents aren't perfect, nor are excellent leaders, but both understand that there are no shortcuts to successful family or workplace lives. Just as common sense and good judgment form the foundation for sound parenting decisions, these attributes are necessary for solid management decisions. Good parents love to parent. Good leaders love to lead.

Examples of How Good Mothering Skills Translate Into Maternalism

Just as a good mother:	A maternalistic leader:
Teaches her child to look both ways before crossing the street . . .	Provides education and training before asking an associate to take on a new or foreign task.
Allows her child to tie his shoes once he's learned how (and no longer ties them for him) . . .	Allows associates to be responsible, and does not rescue them or "take over" their jobs when the going gets rough.
Would allow her sixteen-year-old more independence than she would give to her five-year-old . . .	Encourages the autonomy and independence of more mature and proven associates.
Disciplines to teach and to change behavior, not to belittle or harm the self-esteem of her child . . .	Takes corrective (disciplinary) action aimed at informing associates and changing their behavior, not to "punish" or attack self-worth.
Balances the needs of the individual child with the needs of the entire family . . .	Balances the needs of the individual associate with the needs of the entire company.

Just as a good mother:	A maternalistic leader:
Models behavior for her children . . .	Models behavior for his or her associates.
Takes an active interest in her children's education . . .	Takes an active interest in his or her associates' education.
Can make a decision for the good of her child even when the child is unable to recognize her wisdom (and perhaps resents the decision) . . .	Can make a decision for the good of associates who might not have the information or experience to appreciate the decision (and who perhaps even resent it).
May ask for input from children in planning the family vacation, or seek consensus on the choice of a restaurant for dinner, but directs the children's moral and ethical decisions . . .	Follows own discretion to use input, consensus, and authoritarian directives at different times, in different situations.
Knows she's human and that she makes mistakes, is able to admit to not always being right, and knows that she can learn from her children . . .	Knows that he or she is human and makes mistakes, is able to admit to not always being right, and is willing to learn from associates.

The Twelve Tenets of Maternalistic Management

Like all theories, the theory of Maternalistic Management is founded on certain basic principles. Any individual who wishes to lead with love must have a clear understanding of the following twelve tenets of maternalism.

1. Maternalism evokes the idea of mothering, but is not the same thing as "Mama Management."

2. Maternalism implies an ability to see and work for the long-term good.

3. Maternalism includes a recognition that relationships change over time.

4. Maternalism includes a recognition that not all people must be treated exactly alike.

5. Maternalistic leaders aren't competing for popularity.

6. Maternalism involves both role modeling and mentoring.

7. Maternalism is evidenced by respectful love— even during discipline.

8. Maternalistic leaders are aware of their own and others' strengths and weaknesses.

9. Maternalistic leaders know when to let go.

10. Maternalistic leaders take pleasure in watching associates succeed—even when their success surpasses that of the leaders.

11. Maternalistic leaders understand and honor traditions and ceremonies.

12. Maternalistic leaders don't abdicate leadership.

1. Maternalism evokes the idea of mothering, but is not the same thing as "Mama Management."

While "Mama" rushes in to solve everyone's problems (thereby keeping them immature and dependent), a maternalistic manager embodies what many counselors and psychologists would label "good parenting." The good mother cares for, guides, and supports dependent children, but bases her guidance and support on the underlying goal of raising mature, well-balanced, independent adults. She allows her children to take risks, but only after she's given them the education and tools necessary for success. When they fail at something, she's there to pick them up, dust off their jeans, praise them for trying, reinforce or add to their education, give them encouragement, and start them off to try again (on either the same path or another).

You've probably heard the saying, "We must give our children two special things . . . one is roots, and the other is wings." A maternalistic leader, like a good mother, gives both of these things to her associates: a supportive environment (roots) and the tools to become independent (wings). She provides education and opportunities to learn as she shares her own knowledge and experience.

Mahatma Gandhi demonstrated a trait of maternalistic leadership. He knew that solving problems for his countrymen was not the loving thing to do. He said, "If you give a poor man ten rupees you will feed him for the next meal. If you teach him how to sow his own food, he becomes an altogether different man."

2. Maternalism implies an ability to see and work for the long-term good.

Mothering starts out with this premise from the very beginning: who would ever willingly go through the pain of childbirth if there was not to be a reward at the end? (Not only does the pain go away, but when it does there is that beautiful baby!) Much of good parenting demands that the easier route be forsaken for the harder way that will bring a more rewarding future. Sure, it might be easier to let the television baby-sit than to take the time to talk or read with the children, but what kind of teenager and adult results from this abdication of vital parental interaction? Good parenting means being willing to spend hours dealing with children and their developmental needs, knowing that the eventual outcome will be successful adults.

Similarly, maternalistic leaders in organizations are willing to sacrifice short-term objectives for the greater long-term good of the organization and its stakeholders. Norman Vincent Peale demonstrated this maternalistic mindset when he said, "We need to concentrate on doing worthwhile activities—identifying our problems, large and small, in priority order . . . identifying their root causes, and then working to solve them. That will mean giving up immediate pleasures. But if we don't voluntarily make these changes now—in the short run—we certainly will have to in the long run."

3. Maternalism includes a recognition that relationships change over time.

In a family, the dynamics between the parents and their children progress over time. It is only logical that a healthy relationship between a mother and her child will change during that child's infancy, toddler stage, childhood, adolescence, and adulthood. At each stage, the child becomes more independent, until the time when there are two adults (parent and child) who can support and learn from each other.

Similarly, a maternalistic leader has a changing relationship with associates. As an organizational member grows in his or her position through education, experience, expanded responsibility, and the assuming of authority, healthy leader-employee dynamics will change from the earlier roles to interdependent collegial relations.

Motivation is much studied and talked about in management courses and literature. Maslow's Hierarchy of Needs (mentioned in Chapter One) is often used to explain different levels of needs that motivate adult workers. The same model is used in pediatric textbooks to describe human development! Writers use this theory to illustrate changing motivations, and because it appears intuitively correct it is accepted for both child and adult development. Good parents understand the levels of fulfillment needed by their children; good managers know the levels needed to motivate adults at work. Both recognize that with education and in a supportive environment, any developing human (child or associate) will grow and change, need different things from parents or leaders at different stages, be motivated by different rewards, and progress from immaturity to maturity.

4. Maternalism includes a recognition that not all people must be treated exactly alike.

Any involved parent knows that each of his or her children is an individual. Try as we might to treat all of our kids "the same," it isn't possible, because no two children are the same. Their drives, talents, judgment, interests, maturity, intelligence, rates of development, and emotional stability differ. What motivates them also differs. Good parenting means recognizing these differences and adjusting the parenting approach according to the child.

Adults, too, have different needs, personalities, and ways of reacting to their environment. They have different abilities and skill levels. Good managers recognize the differences and adapt to them. While the leader's behavior is governed by certain underlying principles such as ethics, empathy, and a positive regard for others, these principles are manifested in differing ways, according to the situation. One important consideration is the individual associate. A manager might delegate a certain task to employee A and not to employee B, even though both employees have the same job description. Why? Because employee A has a greater interest in that particular task, is more skilled in that regard, or has the kind of personality best suited to the task.

In today's business environment, some employees are more than ready for the current push to self- or shared governance, others need education and guidance before they'll be ready, and still others may never be ready.

5. Maternalistic leaders aren't competing for popularity.

Is there an involved parent anywhere who never hears hateful, angry words from his or her offspring? Part of a parent's job is to make decisions for a child and for the family, and those decisions will not always be greeted with joy or even acceptance. Conflict, and sometimes disobedience, results when children don't agree with Mom's or Dad's rulings. The good parent makes the decision he or she believes to be right nonetheless, remembering that the main objective is to be a good parent, not a popular friend. This sometimes means having to resort to discipline.

The good manager follows the same principles. She knows that management is not a popularity contest. Her decisions are based on what is best for the company, the customers, and the employees. Her effort to balance the needs of these different groups dictates that not everyone can be happy with every decision she makes, and this she accepts. Since universal pleasure with her decisions isn't attainable, for her it isn't even a worthwhile goal. Like the parent, she tries to do what is right, based on her conscience, her best judgment, and all available information. And sometimes she, too, must resort to discipline.

6. Maternalism involves both role modeling and mentoring.

Parents are the primary role models for their children. (In our culture, we recognize this particularly when lamenting the lack of father figures in so many single-parent homes.) We know that little girls learn how to be women by watching their mothers. Little boys grow up to be men by observing their fathers. Parenting is copied from one generation to the next. Either actively (by reflecting about what they're doing) or passively (just by being the ones that the children most

> *Politics asks the question, "Is it expedient?"*
> *Vanity asks, "Is it popular?" But conscience*
> *asks, "Is it right?"*
> — Martin Luther King, Jr.

observe), parents are responsible for guiding their children to adulthood. Just as management ideas abound, so do theories and methods for parenting—from the widely read Dr. Spock to current ideas like Parent Effectiveness Training.

Managers, too, are role models in their organizations. Junior managers pattern their careers after senior bosses that they see as successful or admirable. The top leader's behavior sets the norms for the entire organization. The boss may choose active mentoring (by selecting promising juniors to aid and guide) or passive mentoring (by making no deliberate selection of mentees, yet still providing guidance and help to others in achieving career goals).

Maternalistic managers are aware of role modeling and mentoring. They consciously model behavior for others in the organization. They actively mentor associates and provide help to all employees who want to develop new skills.

7. Maternalism is evidenced by respectful love — even during discipline.

Good parents understand that discipline is sometimes necessary. They know the difference between the child and his behavior. That is, corrective action (discipline) taken when a child misbehaves is aimed toward behavior, not the child himself. Discipline is not personal; the child is not loved any less because he was corrected.

Maternalistic leaders understand that there is a difference between the worth of an associate as a person and his behavior at work. When an employee must be counseled or disciplined, the communication from the manager is about the behavior (performance or work habits) that needs to change or improve. The communication does not take away from the intrinsic value of the associate as a human being. Even when taken to its ultimate form, the termination (firing) of an individual, the discipline is about behaviors such as poor performance or poor work habits, and is never a personal attack.

Both children and adults may at times need discipline, but with maternalism it is accomplished in a respectful way.

8. Maternalistic leaders are aware of their own and others' strengths and weaknesses.

To truly love means to love in spite of imperfections. In parenting lingo, this is expressed as the need for children to receive unconditional positive regard. That is, they are loved by their parents even when they've acted in an unlovable manner. Their behavior may be unworthy of high regard, but they themselves are worthy of being cared for. Similarly, a maternalistic leader holds others in high esteem, even when their actions are not esteemed.

The maternalistic leader sets high standards for himself and others, but he understands that there is no such thing as a perfect person. All people fail at times to meet standards. Because he realizes this, the maternalistic leader is able to show kindness and forgiveness both to others and to himself. He can then give honest feedback without provoking defensiveness, and can accept it as well. This is an essential ability if he is to help himself and others learn and grow.

Theories abound about how a team's accomplishments can equal much more than the sum of its individual members' accomplishments. But this can happen only if the different strengths of each team member are fully recognized and utilized. As intuitively correct as team synergy theory is, its promise cannot be realized if this recognition doesn't happen. Maternalistic leaders know this. An acknowledgment of any weak areas is the first step in formulating a plan to strengthen them. By recognizing strengths and weaknesses, the good leader can bring together and coordinate teams of people so that their synergy is magnified.

9. Maternalistic leaders know when to let go.

There are lots of jokes in our society about the mom who never lets her kids grow up. In the name of love, she clings to her children, interferes with their decisions, tries to control their lives. The adult son living with "Mama" in a codependent state is an American cliché, and we usually see this kind of mother as a poor parent.

The good mother raises her children to be successful on their own. According to Dorothy Rich, author of the parenting book *Mega Skills,* parents have the job of helping their kids develop caring, effort, teamwork, confidence, motivation, perseverance, initiative, responsibility, common sense, and problem solving. So it should be a mother's goal to produce mature, successful, self-sufficient adults, and when the young adults are ready for independence, the wise mother lets go.

The maternalistic leader is responsible for providing learning opportunities for associates, as well as help in developing caring, effort, teamwork, confidence, motivation, perseverance, initiative, responsibility, common sense, and problem solving! The manager's goal is to produce mature, successful, self-sufficient associates, and when this has been done, he or she lets go. Letting go means no more micro-management—the giving up of power and control. Letting go means delegation, empowerment, and the sharing of authority, based on trust in the associates' maturity and ability.

10. Maternalistic leaders take pleasure in watching associates succeed—even when their success surpasses that of the leaders.

One of the greatest joys a parent can feel is in seeing a child triumph, succeed, do well in life. Whether it's a straight-A report card, a lead in the school play, graduation from college, or an outstanding career, the child's success reflects on the parent. Included in the mother's and father's love is the desire for their offspring to excel and to be recognized for their excellence, whether or not their own parenting is credited for the son's or daughter's success.

Similarly, maternalistic managers find that one of their greatest career rewards is those times when their associates excel. Writer Alan McGinnis said this in 1985: "There is simply no substitute for the rewards of helping other people grow, the pleasures of teaching other people to succeed, and the excitement of organizing a group of colleagues." Wess Roberts, author of *Leadership Secrets of Attila the Hun*, said it another way in 1993: "A Chieftain's greatest reward lies in helping Huns and Warriors prosper. Enjoying the personal prosperity a Chieftain acquires is only a secondary pleasure." It is not unusual for individuals to be unaware of how others have contributed to their triumphs, yet a maternalistic leader takes pleasure in an associate's success even when her guidance is not recognized as a contributing factor!

11. Maternalistic leaders understand and honor traditions and ceremonies.

Sociologists have long been aware of the importance of both tradition and ceremony. They understand that customs, stories, and even mythology bind people together in a shared culture. Strong families and strong tribes have strong traditions. They participate in specific ceremonies. They share customs long after the origin of those customs is forgotten. Maternalistic leaders realize that the inhabitants of workplaces have an equally strong need for tradition if they are to unite as a loyal work family.

> *Some old employees of [a major airline] still speak about the days when the company felt like a family, when there was a mutual loyalty between management and the front-line workers. When our old CEO was here and an employee had a baby, the company presented the family with a baby blanket. Now we don't even get a card. Where's the baby blanket? I'll tell you where the loyalty is: in the dumpster.*
>
> – An employee, reminiscing about tradition

Company traditions might be as simple as an annual Christmas party or a summer picnic. They might be some sort of recognition of individual milestones like birthdays or company anniversary dates. Anything that employees can learn to expect and look forward to becomes a company custom. The importance of each tradition should not be overlooked or underestimated, for when a tradition is not continued, there may be subtle or obvious weakening of the company's foundation of employee loyalty.

12. Maternalistic leaders don't abdicate leadership.

No matter how mature the children, no matter how democratic the family, as long as people live together as a family, good parenting requires parents who retain the leadership roles. Organizations of people, whether they are families, tribes, nations, or companies, require ultimate decision makers and direction setters. Otherwise, we'd have a kind of familial anarchy, and—because we all have different goals, needs, and personalities—major decisions that affect the entire group might never be made. Sometimes parents must be directive.

It would seem to be common sense that bosses need to be managers in the basic sense of the word. Yet some executives who see themselves as loving, participative, enlightened leaders, believe that they should never have to give directions, that associates or groups of employees can come to consensus about every aspect of business.

It is not human nature for all of us to agree all of the time. There are times when consensus is appropriate and other times when nothing but management edict will do.

Comprehending this reality is one hallmark of the loving leader.

Thus, maternalistic leaders don't forget that they are the leaders. No matter how able or mature the associates, no matter how democratic, supportive, and nurturing the work environment, companies still need managers. Bosses are still essential as bosses—the planners, organizers, coordinators, and decision makers. They are that place where the buck stops. The best leaders, like the best parents, exhibit courage, strong character, a sense of humor, and the ability to confront. Roles may change with the times, but the need for strong leaders in organizations continues.

The Continuing Need for Managers

Maternalism includes the essential recognition that even the most mature group of associates needs formal leaders. The question is: What do we need them for?

Skills that are considered prerequisites to management jobs are based on what various "gurus" have determined that managers do. An army of consultants has grown up around the concepts that (1) companies are only as good as their management team, (2) it's possible to determine the specific skills that are important to any managerial job, (3) it's possible to measure how competently managers complete their skills, and (4) it's possible to teach management skills.

What are these skills of management, so needed in a rapidly changing world? In order to answer that question, a more basic query must first be made: What is it that managers do? And is whatever they do today what they should be doing tomorrow?

Certain tasks have traditionally been assigned to managers, whether they be managers of a home, a business, or a country. These tasks include planning, controlling, organizing, decision making, managing change, managing conflict, and interfacing with the system's environment.

Planning: In any given organization, most of the employees will take it for granted that their formal leaders, the bosses, have a plan for the company. (They might believe that these are deep, dark, unpleasant blueprints for the future, but all the same they assume that there are plans.) Business consultants and management schools have taught for years that organizations should have short-term, medium-term, and long-term plans. What is happening these days is that the gap between "long-term" and "what we'd better be doing *right now* if we plan to be here tomorrow" is getting more and more narrow. Planning requires forecasting the future, and—even in the best of times—crystal balls are not crystal clear. These days the slush makes them murky indeed. People who do their jobs far removed from the hallowed halls of executivedom would probably be surprised at the fluidity of plans currently being made, and at the uncertainty among top management about appropriate courses to follow. Bosses are not wizards; their consultants are not seers. While they may have more access to trends and to some of the other information necessary for making "informed" estimates, their view of the future is a "guesstimate," however accurate their past track record for planning.

"Planning for the future? What planning?" said a corporate executive with the official title "Planner," adding, "We're trying to adjust to what's happening to us today, and what happened yesterday. Long-term planning used to go years into the future. Now we're lucky if we have definite plans for the next twelve months, with just a general idea of where we're going after that."

Planning is more difficult than it's ever been, and it has a considerably diminished horizon. With all the shifting and uncertainty in the world, more than one leader may be tempted to throw up her hands and ask, "Why even *bother* to plan?"

But however more difficult it is, and whatever the uncertainties, planning remains essential to any organization. It also remains in the management team's domain, because the leaders are the ones most able to gather information, monitor trends, examine forecasts, and both see and interact with the environment. Others in the organization will contribute —in fact, *must* contribute—to planning, but those most responsible (and in the best position to be responsible) are the organization's managers. It is their responsibility to plan for the organization's future. That includes both setting goals and drawing up the blueprints for meeting those goals.

Decision Making: In all arenas of business and government, decisions need continually to be made. Some may seem fairly insignificant (Shall we carpet the lobby in blue or green?), while others obviously have far-reaching implications for the survival of the entity (Shall we stop making large expensive automobiles and concentrate on developing solar-driven, two-person cars?). Whatever the scope of the determination to be made, decision making is an essential management skill.

In a stable and slow-moving world, it might seem easy to choose a course of action. Data can be gathered and formatted into information, forecasting can be done, marketing studies can be completed, and the experts at decision making can look at graphs, numbers, and decision charts before determining their choices. But, even in stable times, forecasting the future is not the science some analytical types would like to believe. Decisions are risky because they must be based on incomplete or less-than-perfect information. Every decision involves the risk that the best choice may not be made.

Today and in the future, because of the instability of the times, the risks look even greater. How does one get a firm enough grasp on today or on projections of tomorrow when one is sliding on slush? Yet decisions must be made, and the time margin for making them is increasingly narrow for organizations and for those leaders who don't want to be left behind in the obsolete zone.

Unfortunately, examples of poor decision-making skills abound:

> Decisions? Yes, those bureaucrats make some pretty dumb decisions. We're always getting new orders about how things are going to get done down here. They're so complicated and unreal that it's obvious they don't know a thing about what we do here. Sometimes there's one decision that comes down one week with an opposite plan the next week. Why don't they ask us? We're doing the job, if they'd just let us do it.
>
> – Loading dock worker
> for a government agency

The worst CEO I ever had was the nicest guy you could ever want to meet. He was friendly with everybody. Problem was he agreed with everybody. Here we were with an industry in crisis and he went around being Mr. Nice Guy, but wouldn't make a decision about ANYTHING. I don't know if he was afraid to decide or he just wanted everybody to like him, but in the end nobody wanted him as the boss because the decisions he wouldn't make made everybody's life miserable—and led to the downfall of the company.

— Executive, private industry

My worst experience was working for a bean counter! You've never been frustrated until your boss is one of these "let's gather all the facts first" guys. The deadlines for making decisions just kept going by, but he wouldn't decide. He just kept asking for "more data, more data"—talk about paralysis by analysis!

— Middle manager, private industry

Being able to make decisions today requires good analytical skills combined with experience, broad sources of information, a dose of intuition, a dash of forecasting (a fairly clear crystal ball), and a great deal of courage. The decision making is easier in organizations where risks are permitted, even encouraged, and mistakes are not automatically terminal to a career. (The companies of today that don't permit risks won't be here tomorrow . . . but that's a subject for Chapter Three.) Whatever the prevailing risk tolerance, it falls to the leaders to make decisions.

Organizing: This book is about organizations, which—by their very name—imply "organization." That is, they are arranged in some sort of administrative structure, with a system that divides labor and dictates who will do what. The term implies an order, the opposite of which could be anarchy or disorder.

Leaders are responsible for "organizing the organization." They set up the infrastructure and systems that they believe will best ensure their company's survival and its ability to meet its objectives. Their goal in this organization is to design an arrangement that is productive, effective, efficient, and adaptive to change. An additional goal is that the organization's structures should encourage the provision of value to its stakeholders.

Typically, organizations have drawn charts to depict their formal organization. These charts are made available to employees so that visual learners can understand how they fit into the overall system. The classical chart is in the form of a pyramid, with the CEO at the top and many workers at the base. In these more democratic times, companies have redesigned themselves and drawn a variety of creative pictorials to describe their organizational relatedness.

It's up to the corporate leaders to determine what this chart will be, and to organize all systems. Does that mean that nonmanagement staff have no role in organizing their work or day-to-day functions? Of course not! Every person in the organization has an organizing role of some nature. But it is the leader who is responsible for seeing that formal organization occurs, that duplication is minimized, that everyone knows their roles.

Controlling: Most people in this country don't like the idea of being controlled by anyone else. After all, we're the nation of democracy and rugged individualism! Probably the distaste we express for anyone called a "boss" has less to do with the individual styles and personality traits of managers than with the very idea that these people have been placed in positions to regulate us. This aversion to being dominated by authority figures causes a few working people to develop a sort of permanent adolescence—a rebellion against anything that smacks of management direction.

Recent management thinking has evolved to theories that call for more "coordinating" and less "directing." The theories make intuitive sense to democratic managers and professors, and to their mature associates. These egalitarians assume that everyone in the organization will be delighted with the idea of more control over their own work life. They're right . . . to some extent. The caveats to their ideas are that (1) along with control comes responsibility and accountability, and (2) not every associate is yet mature enough to

> *The president of Eaton Corporation, Alexander M. Cutler, remarking on his company's culture of empowerment: "The admission ticket for this kind of responsibility is accountability—and not everyone necessarily wants accountability." Some people think they want to be self-directed but discover they can't live up to their part of the bargain.*
>
> — Timothy Aeppel,
> THE WALL STREET JOURNAL

want either the control or the accompanying accountability. Many can gain this maturity with maternalistic management, but some will never choose to take the responsibility.

Even with a very mature workforce, led by a manager who coordinates independent work teams, there is a need for someone who has the official authority to assume control. Situations occur in all walks of life that require a leader to take the reins. Imagine some of these scenarios:

1. You are a passenger on a 747 that is experiencing in-flight mechanical difficulties. Would you prefer that the captain calls together a group made up of co-pilot, flight engineer, and flight attendants for a committee decision, or that the captain maintains control of the plane and directs what will be done?

2. Your company's product is rapidly becoming obsolete. Many employees have ideas about new products the company can make, but you don't have the resources or capacity to make all of them. Would you prefer that the organization's executives spend months arguing while your finances move further into the red, or that the CEO takes control, ensures that a decision is made, and takes prompt action?

3. You are a hospital patient, having your appendix surgically removed or having a heart attack or suddenly unable to breathe. Would you prefer that the doctors, nurses, and other staff have a committee meeting to discuss how to care for you, or that one professional takes control, gives directions, and ensures that your life is preserved?

4. You work in a business important to the public, one that must stay open on holidays. No one who works there wants to work holidays. Would you prefer that no one shows up to work on Memorial Day, or that a boss takes control and ensures that some are scheduled to work that day?

Control remains a leader's job because humans, being human, do not agree 100 percent of the time. Indeed, we don't want people always to agree. Total agreement within an organization is a symptom that the diversity essential to creativity is missing. There are times, though, when consensus and group decision making is too time-consuming or is for some other reason not an option, and that's when managers are needed to take charge. The best leaders delegate control as much as possible, but recognize the need to maintain responsibility and to resume control when the situation requires them to. Strength and forcefulness are still needed, and there are times when nothing less than take-charge management will do.

Managing Conflict: Hand in hand with the occasional duty of taking control is conflict management. Both responsibilities are necessary because of the variety of human resources enriching every organization. The differences among people invariably lead to conflict—which is good, because some organizations do die from a lack of conflict. Their "group think" leads to stagnation, and they get run over by the competition. The flip side is that we don't usually find conflict pleasant. Not many of us truly enjoy worksite arguments. Many of us have been socialized to avoid disagreements, to turn away from confrontation. (The exceptions are those who do like to "play the devil's advocate" or who see every discussion as a high school debate, an opportunity to "win" and "score" over opponents with opposing views.)

The underlying concepts of conflict management are that: (1) organizational members will not always agree and (2) conflict is not a bad thing for a company, because differing opinions can lead to better, more creative solutions to problems. However, unmanaged conflict can also tear a group apart and paralyze an organization. Leaders are responsible for setting the rules about how conflict can be expressed and addressed. As the ultimate decision makers, they are also the tie-breakers.

Managing Change: Just as unmanaged conflict can paralyze an organization, so can unmanaged change. In these days of slush, the number and rapidity of an organization's system mutations, alterations, and modifications can be mind-boggling. Managers find themselves responsible for implementing changes determined by higher management, as well as for recommending and initiating change themselves. Human beings do not welcome change unless they understand it and see it as offering a potential for gain. Otherwise, change is perceived as a disruption, a feared unknown, or a threat of loss. Managers are responsible for minimizing the losses, and explaining and amplifying the gains. An important part of their job is to minimize the organizational disruption and pain that can result from change.

Interacting With the Environment: Organizations can be thought of as systems, or as subsystems in the larger systems of the business community, society, or world. However they are pictured, they have the characteristics of an open system. They must interact with other systems in their environment, including community systems, legal systems, political systems, and business systems. Within these other systems are those who may be supporters, customers, suppliers, regulators, competitors, and rule enforcers.

Someone in the organization must interact with these environmental forces. Someone must represent the organization, communicate with those outside of it, ensure that legal and regulatory mandates are being met, and lobby for the organization's best interest. There may be team members with official titles who do many of these interaction tasks. They may work in marketing, personnel, public relations, or the legal department, but they don't represent the company the way its top manager does. Formal organization leaders are symbols to the outside world, representing what the company is all about.

The Attributes of Leadership

So managers plan, make decisions, organize, control, manage conflict, manage change, interact with the environment, and represent the organization. Because we still need such management work to be done, we still need—and will continue to need in the future—responsible leaders to do these management jobs.

As has been shown, part of all these tasks is the underlying job of coordinating everything that goes on, both within the system and in its interface with the environment. All of these activities call for certain necessary management skills, but even those skills do not amount to sufficient qualification for leadership. Leadership requires more than task ability; it requires leadership attributes.

Given that managers will continue to be a crucial part of organizations, what attributes do our leaders need? Consultants, management writers, and university professors often share, through their lectures and writing, their ideas about what type of leadership is needed today and in the future. What's interesting about much of what is being written in the 1990s is its uniformity. Educators and writers from various industries are talking about the same things: leaders who have integrity, pursue quality, practice empowerment, encourage innovation, are comfortable with change, and have a commitment to or "passion" for their company or product. Future-management profiles are based on what futurists predict for organizations: nondifferentiated workers, the end of traditional hierarchies, and the emergence of multifunctional work teams.

> For your organization to be successful in the future, executives and managers at every level must become more effective leaders . . . the transforming leaders know how to listen to others, actively foster employees' participation, and solicit alternative solutions . . . they continually seek data and ideas.
>
> – Ellen Marszalek-Gaucher and Richard Coffey, TRANSFORMING HEALTHCARE ORGANIZATIONS

Much that nowadays passes for managerial skill won't fit the bill . . . the new masters of coordination [managers] will be paid . . . for their ability to make others feel they care.

— Walter Kiechel III, "How We
Will Work in the Year 2000,"
FORTUNE, 5/17/93

In the New American Hospital, the executive's job becomes that of listener, facilitator, integrator, servant, and visionary.

— V. Clayton Sherman, CREATING THE
NEW AMERICAN HOSPITAL

There's going to be a radical shift in how we feel about managers and organizations. The paradigm is empowerment of customers, managers, and workers. There will be concern for individual dignity, worth, and growth.

— Warren Bennes, THE LEADERSHIP
CHALLENGE (paraphrased)

What are the implications of *not* producing leaders of this type in our organizations? We'd better produce them, or else. Or else what? Or else we get left behind in the global economy, we escalate the perceived boss-worker gulf, we perpetuate a workplace of fear, unhappiness, and mediocrity, we lose our most valuable human resources, and we just generally get stuck in the slush.

We know that current leadership has not inspired widespread trust. We know that people want to be cared about: it is an intrinsic human need to be valued and supported.

If you believe what the evidence shows about our current corporate leaders and managers at all levels, it's obvious that a major advance in leadership thinking is vital to our national interest. The management theories emerging today emphasize that a new style of leadership is needed. As was discussed in Chapter One, many people are equating that style with traits long considered feminine. There is a growing realization that women more naturally demonstrate the characteristics that will be needed in leaders of the future.

Gender is not a determinant of management skill, but the skills of a good parent are. Competent mothers have the skills needed for future leadership because maternalism comes naturally to them. But individuals of either gender—even those who've never parented—can learn to be maternalistic leaders . . . and that's what the following chapters are all about.

*L*oving the Organization

The aim of the person is not to be detached,
but to be more attached.

— Robert Bly

What exactly is an organization? One common definition is that it is something organized that is made up of parts that contribute to the functioning of the whole. With the possible exception of a few people living cloistered existences, every person on earth belongs to organizations; families, schools, clubs, churches, companies, sororities, and nations are just some examples.

The organizations known as institutions or companies have common attributes. They are organized in some rational manner, and are made up of parts that become more complex with increasing company size. These parts may be individuals, work teams, departments, or divisions, but all are components joined in some manner to work for the good of the institution—and all, as we shall explore in this chapter, are in their own way lovable.

Organizations are known to have characteristics and even personalities. Mention IBM or Boeing (or your own place of business) and certain traits come immediately to mind. For small businesses, the personality of the place may be perceived as the personality of the owner, but in larger organizations the personality is unique to the company. CEOs may come and go, but the public perception of the company's image remains largely unchanged.

Perceptions about organizations engender feelings about them, distinct and separate from feelings about their human populations. In fact, organizations get talked about as if they were people. As the following examples show, they are even quoted!

From page 1 of *The Wall Street Journal*, 8/17/94:

K-Mart said it plans to sell majority stakes . . .

United Airlines said it will hire more than 1700 employees . . .

Compaq Computer said it will place warning labels . . .

General Motors said it won't resume imports of the Geo Storm . . .

AMR Corp's American Airlines recently said it will cut 5000 jobs . . .

Organizational entities are discussed as if they think, feel, and judge. They have attributed to them morals (or a lack of them) and motives (such as greed or revenge). They arouse emotions. People may say that they are grateful to the Salvation Army, that they distrust a certain bank, that they even hate a company that they feel has wronged them.

Aren't such comments really about the leadership team of an organization, the people heading the company? Well, no,

. . . and yes. No because, as was stated above, leadership can come and go in an institution without a change in the basic personality or the widespread feelings about it. Yes because, over time, it is the leadership that has the most influence on a company's personality.

If we think of companies as having personalities, we also tend to ascribe to them other human characteristics. In fact, organizations are very much like living organisms: living, breathing entities variously described by their strengths and weaknesses. And, like other organisms, organizations have life cycles.

The Life Cycle of an Organization

A life cycle can be defined as the successive events in the life history of an organism. The human life cycle, for example, is usually said to consist of conception, the prenatal and neonatal phases, infancy, childhood, adolescence, early and middle adulthood, old age, and death.

The life cycle of an organization can be described in a similar manner. The idea for an organization is conceived; the organization is born; it grows, develops, and changes over time. Then, when it is no longer able to adapt in a manner necessary for survival in a changing environment, it dies. Some organizations, such as the Shaker religion, can exist for only a short while; others, such as the Catholic Church, may survive for centuries. Even organizations as large as nations have cycles. Empires rise and empires fall . . .

Why are individual organizations conceived and born? Because they were perceived as being able to meet a need. Why do they continue to exist? Because they continue to meet needs. Why do they cease to exist? Because they no longer meet needs. They have failed to adapt to changing needs, or perhaps aren't able to meet needs as well as a competitor does.

Governments exist to control and administer public policy for national groups. They are supposed to work for the good of the whole country. Churches exist to meet spiritual and social needs. Why do work organizations exist? The answer to that depends on where the organization is in its life cycle.

Conception and Birth

Companies can be born only when two factors are present: (1) there is a perceived need that a new organization could meet, and (2) there is a perceived benefit to the people who start the company. The need might be being met by current business ventures, but the new business is conceived to compete with them, based on a belief that the new product or service will somehow be better. (If a new restaurant opens in a town full of restaurants, it is because the owner believes it will attract customers because it's different: it has better food, service, or entertainment, or it can claim a superior location or ambience.)

Just as it wouldn't make sense to invest time and capital in a venture not thought to be needed (or "wanted," another type of "needed"), it isn't practical to give birth to a new organization unless the founder(s) can expect to benefit from that organization's existence. Truly altruistic institutions might be thought of as exceptions to this rule. For example, a nonprofit organization set up to serve the poor might not be of financial benefit to the people who found the organization, but the founders benefit nonetheless. Benefits to founders aren't all financial. They can also consist of such intangible but "warm, fuzzy" things as personal growth, the fulfillment of a need to be needed, or feelings of worth and of contributing to society. Some entrepreneurs begin their enterprises out of their own needs to strive, to create, or to be challenged.

Charitable organizations aside, the benefit of a business is most often considered to be financial. People who start businesses want some sort of financial gain for the work they put into their companies. Privately held businesses seek this financial gain for the owners, and publicly owned companies seek it for the stockholders. But others gain from the business as well: the employees, related businesses (like suppliers), and the community (because of expanded services or an increased tax base). A business, once born, is of benefit to many—including, of course, its customers.

Growth and Maturity

Like a living organism, the business moves on in its life cycle, from birth to growth and maturity. Some entrepreneurial-type people are only excited about an organization through its birth and early growth period. That's because they enjoy the risks, challenges, and excitement of the earliest days. The early days are reminiscent of the stages of childhood, in that they offer an infinite variety of new experiences.

During growth, the organization is actually evolving. It may become bigger in size, with increasing numbers of products, customers, and employees. It may change form or structure. Growth means that the company is meeting needs, and that it is adapting to new needs in a changing world.

Growing can also mean maturing. Mature companies are those that have been around for a while. They have established reputations and proven track records. Often they are well-trusted because they have shown themselves to be dependable.

The personality of a company changes as the organization matures. The youthful, growing business may seem to be high-energy, hectic, exciting, and somewhat disorganized. The mature company may appear calm, organized, and dignified.

In these days of constant change, some people take comfort in going to work for a mature organization, surmising that it is a safer place to be. But actually, if a business has reached maturity and feels like a safe, risk-free environment, it could be headed for trouble. The world is changing, and with change come altered needs. In order to meet those altered needs, an organization must continually evolve.

We recognize this necessity to evolve in living organisms, including ourselves: the person who stops growing (by ceasing production of new protoplasm cells) is doomed to die; failure to evolve in an evolutionary world means death. In this, the organization is not different from biological beings:

+ The end of its growth means the end of its existence.

+ When it dies, sometimes the end is rapid and seems to come as a great shock to the stakeholders. Sometimes the deterioration leading to the final death throes is agonizingly slow and painful.

✦ Organizations, too, suffer from thanatophobia
(fear of death). They seem to want to exist even
if they no longer serve any purpose.

Does the existence of a life cycle mean that the only
future for a mature company is death? No; maturity doesn't
have to mean the end of growth. Even a long-lived, stable
company can continue to evolve if it doesn't get bogged down
in a stuck state.

The Stuck State

Slogging through slush isn't easy, and organizations are
not always able to continue their progression. Sometimes they
get stuck—unable to pull out of the mush and move forward.

How do they get stuck? By falling prey to fear, by a lack
of vision, by being too successful, by giving rise to a surfeit
of bureaucracy, or perhaps through some combination of
all of these.

It's a paradox of business that success begets failure: the
more successful past practices have been for a company, the
less likely it is that any need to change those practices will be
perceived. If it has always worked well and it's working well
now, it is assumed that it will work well in the future. Companies with the "if it ain't broke, don't fix it" attitude see
themselves as strong, stable, and able to continue on a steady
course. The fact is, they're stuck. A certain business "personality" can become so strong in the ego department that it
believes it will live forever without major change. Past and
current success may cause such myopia that a company, or
an entire industry, may be blind to the chaos swirling

around in its environment. A company can be dead before it knows that it was sick, and the diagnosis (a stuck state) won't be known until the autopsy.

Not keeping a finger on the pulse of its environment can be fatal to a company, for survival in a changing world requires knowledge of current events, an ongoing study of trends, projections into the future, and the all-important ability to change. The kind of change required may be anything from a new vision to an entirely new mission statement.

Even if success doesn't blind a business, some organizations have set up such complex hierarchies and divisional structures that they find themselves stuck when there is a desire to move. When ideas must be passed from layer to layer, they may be obsolete before they get through the company's decision-making process. Being too slow to respond to trends is just as deadly as never seeing them. By the time the organization can focus on change and begin the adaptations necessary for survival, it may be too late.

A stuck state can be engendered by frightened leaders. People whose success occurred practicing "the old ways" may be fearful of change because of its risks. Leaders may fear that they will become obsolete if a company's mission or mode of operation changes. One example is the CEO of a midsize service company who refused to computerize his business because he was not computer-literate. His company clung to pen and pencil while competitors left him in the dust with their information systems. Moving quickly though slush requires risk-taking, and settled, successful leaders may be unwilling to take the risks they would have considered while they were "on their way up."

> *An essential quality of a good manager is that he or she deals with bad news head on, seeking it out rather than denying it. An effective manager wants to hear about what's going wrong before what's going right.*
>
> — Bill Gates, founder and CEO,
> Microsoft Corporation

The fear of corporate change is closely related to a fear of conflict. Not all business leaders enjoy hearing a variety of opinions. In fact, some CEOs may be unaware that there are thoughts that differ from theirs. Others may refuse to listen to anything that they perceive as being unpleasant. Consciously or unconsciously, they may send out a message to their working colleagues that it isn't safe to disagree with "upper management," or to bring bad news to the boss. Indeed, too much conflict in a company can paralyze progress, but too little conflict (which represents differing ideas) can be just as lethal. In fact, more organizations die from a *lack* of conflict than from excessive management disagreement. Why? Because conflict is a sign of creativity, and of the recognition by some that there is a need for change. Managers who are uncomfortable with an environment that is not 100 percent pleasant and free of disagreement are dooming their businesses to a permanent freeze, which means being left behind to die.

There is good news about stuck states. With loving leadership, it's possible to get out of them if interventions are taken in time. Even companies that have had "near death" experiences have been resuscitated and have recovered to go

Examples of Company Life Cycles

A youthful, growing company:

new ideas » risk-taking » new products » growth

A mature company (growing in response to changes around it, and profitable today):

new ideas » risk-taking » new products » profitable tomorrow

A mature company (dying in response to change, though profitable today):

no change » no new ideas » no risk » gone tomorrow

on to thriving, productive futures. Just as human organisms can be revived through cardiopulmonary resuscitation, a business can be given new life through its own form of CPR: change, proactivity, and renewal. This can occur when someone sees the light, breathes oxygen into the organization, and gets the company's heart started again, before death is inevitable.

Organizational Death

The endpoint of any life cycle is the cessation of life, and organizational death occurs when an organization no longer fulfills unmet needs. Organizations, like organisms, naturally struggle against that ending. When a company's adaptation and/or evolution isn't keeping pace with the evolving environment, it can be a sad experience to watch that organization slide downhill over time, desperately casting about for an anchor hold. Sometimes, when an organization's mission

Where Is Your Organization in the Life Cycle?

	INFANCY	YOUTH	MATURITY	DECLINE	DEATH
IBM			X		
Ford Motor			X		
Sears			X		
Microsoft		X			
Eastern Airlines					X
Your Company	?	?	?	?	?

or products are no longer of value to its customers or community (whether that be a local community or the world community), "putting the company to sleep" is the only possible recourse. If the products or services are no longer needed, and the organization is unable to remedy this, it is right for the organization to cease its existence. One example of this might be a hospital in a community with multiple hospitals. It may no longer be needed because of changes in healthcare practice and in the area population. Perhaps it is the oldest hospital building in the area, with the oldest technology. The patients it serves can be better served by a newer hospital a few blocks away. Because closing the hospital would decrease costs to the community and increase the quality of patient care, allowing the organization to cease existence would probably be the right thing to do.

The culture of an organization reflects its soul.

– Karleen Kerfoot, nurse executive

Vision, Mission, Goals, and Objectives

These days, there is much talk about the need for leaders with vision, and a great deal is being written about the need for organizations to have a written mission statement, accompanied by strategic planning and formal goals and objectives. This is a good trend, for it is quite true that companies need visionary leadership, and that a written mission statement is a useful starting point for business planning and decisions.

The holding of a vision implies that an organization has a future. The mission statement explains why the organization exists—what needs it meets. Goals and objectives spell out how the vision will be pursued and how the mission will be carried out. Without a shared vision and mission, an organization can't trudge through slush, because the various components of the company may be facing (and moving in) different directions.

It's not enough to have a written mission statement. It is essential that the mission claimed by a company be evidenced by the company's actions. It is necessary that the humans responsible for carrying out actions on behalf of the company understand the mission. Without this understanding and commitment to the mission, it is impossible to love the organization.

Loving the Organization

How can a leader (or a follower, for that matter) love an organization? Isn't that akin to claiming love for an inanimate object? No, for an organization is not an inanimate object. Yes, it may appear to consist of some inanimate

> When I confide that I love the hospital I work in, I'm not just talking about the buildings. I'm expressing affection for the people who work there, the patients who are treated there, the community that is served there. I am passionate about what "my" hospital stands for.
>
> — Nurse executive

bricks and mortar, but it is so much more than that. We have already addressed the fact that companies have personalities, and isn't personality what we really love?

That is how the love of an organization starts: knowing and believing in its mission and understanding its vision and goals. It doesn't matter what type of business or institution the organization is; without leaders and associates who believe in its value, it can never be loved.

Because the values of individuals differ, different people are capable of loving different organizations. For example, it could be easy for a given individual to love and believe in a hospital, but impossible for that same person to love a company that makes cigarettes or chemical weapons. It doesn't matter if the organization is a restaurant, daycare facility, or automobile manufacturer . . . it can't be loved by leaders who don't believe in its mission.

The number-one rule of loving an organization is this: *You must believe in its mission.* If your personal values do not correspond with the company's values, there can be no real bond, and it is not then healthy—for you or for the organization—to continue the relationship. Working for a business does constitute a relationship, which, like any relationship, requires bonding if any sort of commitment is to be made. And a mutual commitment is required if maternalistic management is to emerge.

In maternalistic management, personal values and organizational values match. A leader can love the company only when she can admire it, identify with it, want to protect it, and desire its success. Maternalistic leaders are passionate in their desire for their organizations to succeed.

Successful Organizations

"People want to be associated with a successful organization." This is one of those statements called by this writer an "intuitism," meaning that the statement, like many management theories, can be intuitively accepted at face value as a truism.

What is a successful organization? Most often our Western society defines success in financial terms, which does have some merit as a definition. After all, without some sort of financial success an organization will cease to exist. But there are other measures of business success in addition to revenue. These may include producing a good product, or meeting a need for society. One measure of success can be meeting the needs of customers and employees. And one important measure is simply this: do the managers and their associates feel proud of the company?

It isn't possible to love the organization without feeling pride in it. As was mentioned in the previous section, a manager's pride in an association can only occur when the individual's and the organization's values match. A manager who loves her organization wants it to succeed. More than that, she wants the business to thrive. And, in order to perform in a manner that helps this to occur, she has to be able to balance the organization's success with her own.

Entrepreneurs who start companies see their own success and the organization's as the same thing. This identification makes it possible for them to make tremendous sacrifices for the good of the company. Innumerable success stories from this country's great companies chronicle the beginning days of a business—the days of long hours and small profit while the business was being built.

But what happens when the company becomes financially successful, or when the original entrepreneur turns over the management to professional managers? If those paid leaders don't love the organization as the entrepreneur did, the company story now changes.

American companies are rife with leaders who appear not to love them. These are leadership teams whose personal goals are met at the expense of the company. Rather than see the organization as an organism or a personality to be admired, they see the company as a stage for their successful performances, a place to earn personal fortunes, to shine, to be stars. Their need for personal success outweighs any wishes they might have for the company's success. Does that mean they don't care if the organization is successful? No. They are very concerned about its successes and failures, but only because these reflect on their own luminous careers.

Do these words sound too harsh? Just consider the American business world of today. Some of the enormous salaries paid to top managers can only be called obscene, but few nonfounding, paid managers will admit this or turn down exorbitant wages. Golden parachutes and organization hopping based on personal careers or opportunities for increased income are the order of the day. Some executives are wooed away from one company to share its secrets with a competitor. Other executives can watch their organizations decline, lose market share, and resort to massive personnel layoffs, and then still insist on their own bonuses and special perquisites. Twenty years ago, the CEOs of large American companies made forty times more than their average worker. The current average CEO pay is two hundred times that of the average worker.

To deny that managers should be well paid for superior performance is not this book's purpose. Leaders shouldn't be expected to be completely altruistic in their service to the organization. Their talents should be rewarded. But sometimes the excesses of the rewards are symptoms of a lack of leadership love.

Before losing his job as CEO of New York's Empire Blue Cross and Blue Shield, Albert Cordone took home $600,000 a year. In addition, he had a chauffeur-driven Lincoln Towne Car, took helicopter trips to meetings, had company accounts at Tiffany and Cartier jewelers, a fleet of 123 cars, $132,179 in art and sculpture, $62,832 in silk plants for an office complex, and $46,000 in telecommunications and security systems in his home. The company bought him a $20,000 Chippendale desk.

While Mr. Cordone enjoyed these perks, his nonprofit company was publicly claiming poverty and drastically raising healthcare premiums of the elderly, poor, and chronically ill.

– TIME magazine, 7/12/93

One complaint about American workers is that they see their work as "just a job" and are not dedicated to their company's success. Unloving leaders are no different: they can be lured to jump from company to company solely for their own careers and without consideration for detrimental effects on the organizations. They give the impression that even top leadership is "just a job."

When a position is "just a job," leadership decisions will not be made for the good of the business. In other words, without loving leadership, business decisions may be made for the good of the leaders, at the expense of the organization's good. Thus the company suffers from a lack of loyalty.

Loyalty

Organizations need leaders who are loyal to them. "Loyalty?" you may say. "In this age of temporary arrangements? Of throwaway relationships, short-term employment, and multiple marriages?" In management school, it is being taught that the new generation of Americans will be difficult to manage because of their lack of loyalty. They just aren't committed to their work. Could that be because leaders haven't been committed to their work or organizations either?

Loyalty is a commitment. Without such a commitment from leaders, how can an organization thrive? Loyalty is a part of loving, but it is difficult to describe. It's another one of those things of which people say, "Well, I can't tell you exactly what it is, but I know it when I see it."

If we know it when we see it, what does leadership loyalty look like? It looks like this: the people in charge consider the success of the organization in every decision they make; they speak with pride of their company; they have track records of staying with an organization over time; they will defend it against its competitors; they believe in what it stands for and what it does.

Loving leadership doesn't mean that a manager must demonstrate loyalty by staying with the same organization for his entire working career. Very loyal people have moved from one company to another, even one industry to another. Sometimes these moves are based on the need to balance self-love with organizational love (the move may mean advancement not available in the current organization). Sometimes it's the most loyal thing to do: "I no longer have the drive to do what this company needs. I need to move on so a more appropriate person can replace me." But while the loyal person is part of an organization, his loyalty is with that organization.

Part of leadership loyalty is ensuring that the organization can survive without you. We call that ensuring continuity through succession planning. Another part is preparing for competition and competing with the organization's competitors wholeheartedly. Loyal leaders are those who believe that they and the organization win together.

Among business leaders who are unable to exhibit loyalty are those who suffer from a problem called Leadership Deficit Disorder (LDD). Managers suffering from LDD are too selfish to think of the organization's good as being equal in importance to their own. They have a desire to win whether or not the organization also wins. LDD leaders are "me first" bosses, and their organizations lose out because they are considered a far second.

Loyal or Disloyal Leaders:
We Know Them When We See Them

I once worked for a CEO who was the epitome of the loyal leader. Every decision he made was based on what he felt was right for the organization, even to the choice to leave his job. He explained his early retirement to me this way: "The world is changing and I feel unable to change with it. In order to survive, this company has got to move quickly and I am unable to move as quickly as we should. We need to hire a president with the drive and energy, one who has what I don't have. If I stay here, my conservative ways will be a hindrance, not a help."

I also once worked for a CEO who wasn't loyal. This was apparent to his direct reports (and eventually to others) by his lack of concern for solving problems, for seeking new business opportunities for the company, or for even putting in a full day's work at the office. His slant on everything was how good it made him look, and he spent much of his time cultivating his network so that he'd be able to move into a better job with another organization.

– An industry middle manager

Leadership Deficit Disorder and Other Organizational Ills

If one considers an organization to be a living, breathing organism, one can also think of it in terms of its health. It can be healthy, vital, and growing. It can have a variety of minor aches and pains. Or it can exhibit symptoms of serious illness.

Leadership Deficit Disorder (LDD) is a major disease that can cripple a company. Because good leadership is such an essential ingredient for success, organizations without it are unable to create and grow. Many may point fingers at outside influences such as labor unions, a fickle customer population, or government rules and regulations as reasons for business declines. But in thus trying to assign blame for their company's declining health, they miss one principal pathogen: the pathological leaders.

LDD exists in various forms, since it is possible to be deficient in any or all of numerous leadership abilities such as love, ethics, charisma, intelligence, credibility, technical knowledge, or financial acumen. How critical the disorder is to the well-being of a company depends on what level of management is infected (the higher the level of diseased management, the poorer the prognosis) and how many abilities are missing in the leaders. A manager who isn't very smart but is ethical, credible, and charismatic may do little harm to an institution's health compared to the ravages caused by another highly placed individual with multiple deficits.

One of the most common symptoms of LDD is a basic inability to manage and lead. It is often said in the business community that we need leaders who can "fire us up" with their vision. What is not in demand is the manager who is seen as a plodder—one so immersed in managing details that she can't see the future until it's too late. On the other hand, the grandest plans for the future will never come to fruition if the day-to-day details of running the business are left un-attended.

In biological disease, it is frequently not the primary disorder that causes death, but the secondary conditions created by the primary disorder. For example, a person with diabetes usually doesn't have his death attributed to that primary diagnosis per se, but to disorders caused by the diabetes, such as heart disease, kidney failure, or hypertension. In organizational disease, the secondary illnesses caused by LDD can be lethal. These include DOS (Dysfunctional Organizational Syndrome), BLMI (Bottom Line Mental Illness), AP (Analysis Paralysis), and EDD (Ethics Deficiency Disease).

Three Examples of Ethics Deficiency Disease

Several years ago I worked for a manager who used to travel to New York on business. He always went there with empty suitcases and bought all new suits and clothes, which he charged to his expense account. His rationale was that he needed to look good at out-of-town meetings. When I mentioned to him that I was uncomfortable with this practice and that it looked to me like stealing from the company, or the client, he laughed and said, "You just don't understand Big Biz." In fact, that's the line I always got when I questioned things. It's now a joke around our house: "Big Biz" means dishonesty.

– A former business consultant

I just saw the movie CLEAR AND PRESENT DANGER, and it really made me sad. The president character reminded me of our CEO. He and his advisors made every decision based on their own political agenda, not on what was good for the company or the people. Just like the president sacrificed the lives of soldiers for his career, so does our CEO sacrifice employees to layoffs for his career. I really identified with the Jack Ryan character who was accused of seeing things as "black and white." His reply was, "No, I see them as right or wrong."

– A middle manager

Around here it used to be that any new management jobs were "posted," so that internal candidates could apply, and advertised for outside applicants, too. Then we would interview, and hire the best candidate for the job. Our new CEO doesn't work things that way. It's like he considers every job his personal patronage reward to give away. Jobs aren't posted or advertised. He hires people whom he "owes" or who will gain personal leverage for him. His hires are friends' kids, graduates from his school, members of his organizations, or others who will somehow gain him potential career advantage. Never mind that many he hires are mediocre and not in the best interest of the company. I've been told this is common in business and that men understand this as acceptable, but it makes me sad.

– A female vice president

Ethics Deficiency is a particularly troubling malady because it is difficult to diagnose. Demonstrating ethical behavior is part of loving an organization, yet the distinction between right and wrong seems hard for some bosses to grasp. In a world where politics and compromise are the acceptable modes of making progress, more than a few gray areas of conduct exist. Yet outsiders or others not directly involved are usually able to spot unethical behavior immediately. Certain issues are common ethical dilemmas for managers:

1. Poor quality: putting profits before quality

2. Making misleading claims about products

3. Becoming partners with a less-than-ethical company for good business purposes

4. Personal or company greed

5. Lying or requiring others to lie

6. Unfair policies (favoritism) for promotion, job assignments, equal opportunities, etc.

7. Cover-ups when errors occur

8. Reneging on promises or contracts

9. Disloyalty to the company and/or to co-workers

10. Knowingly providing an unsafe or fraudulent product or service

11. An imbalance of love for customers, employees, company, and self (e.g., putting personal success above that of all others)

12. Price fixing

13. Industrial espionage

14. Practicing "turfism" vs. doing what's right for the entire company

15. Wasting company money or time

16. Failing to speak up and expose unethical practices or behavior

In the culture of the maternal organization, ethics are essential. Even when preparing for competition, maternal leaders send the message that the company will "play fair." Just as children are taught that hitting, biting, lying, and stealing are not acceptable to the family, the company's associates need to know that moral codes are practiced and enforced. Ethical companies don't use dishonest, misleading advertising and they don't resort to industrial spying.

In the following list of organizational maladies, all of the diseases are infectious, and none can be completely healed without loving leadership at the top.

Organizational Disease	Symptoms	Outcomes and Prognosis
Leadership Deficit Disorder (LDD)	Management's lack of attention to the details of running the business, lack of visible concern for its success, and/or lack of skill in guiding and influencing others.	Progresses to other crippling disorders. Infectious throughout organization. Can become chronic malaise leading to eventual organizational death. Cure is possible if deficit is treated with an infusion of loving leadership.

Organiza-tional Disease	Symptoms	Outcomes and Prognosis
Dysfunctional Organizational Syndrome (DOS)	Lack of communication throughout organization. Turfism, wall-building between departments, individual success based on political maneuvering rather than merit. No shared vision. Components duplicating efforts or working at cross purposes. Hyper-criticism, hypoproductivity, defensiveness.	Secondary to LDD. Infectious, contributing to low productivity, indi-vidual burnout, malaise leading to eventual death. Cure is possible if primary disorder (LDD) is treated.
Bottom Line Mental Illness (BLMI)	"The bottom line" is the only criterion for decision-making. Quality of products or services is not held in high esteem.	Short-term financial success, long-term organizational decline following morale problems, quality deficiencies.
Analysis Paralysis	Decisions are not made as data is analyzed repeatedly.	Organizational decline.
Ethics Deficiency Disease (EDD)	Padded expense accounts. Lying. Office supply theft. Cheating customers for a profit.	Decreasing organizational loyalty. Organizational decay and decline.

The Responsibilities of Boards of Directors

If CEOs must be healthy and maternalistic, what are the responsibilities of their bosses, those men and women on the Boards of Directors who have fiduciary and oversight authority in most large businesses?

Organizational boards range from highly compensated groups in big business to volunteers in small charities or nonprofit companies. The individuals who serve on boards may be called directors, trustees, or simply members. Whether or not they are paid (serving on corporate boards can be a lucrative undertaking), they are usually responsible for hiring, evaluating, and paying the CEO. Some boards are more involved than others in the business decisions or policy setting of the company, but all have a responsibility for financial oversight.

One of the problems with a board system is that political maneuvering within such a governing body can bring about decisions that are far removed from an organization's best interest. Another problem is that, while board members may feel that the company owes them something for the time and effort that they put into serving, they may forget that they owe the organization something, too. Acceptance of a board position should not be based purely on money, prestige, or resume building, but on caring for the organization. It is not only the employed management team who must love the organization, but those with governance control as well. Directors, like managers, should believe in the organization's mission, be passionate about its success, have complementary values, show support, and be willing to make decisions that are in the best interest of the organization.

A board member who uses inside information for her own profit to the detriment of the organization does not love that organization. Nor does the director who uses his board position to advance his own causes, no matter how noble, if this is not in the best interest of the organization.

Boards, like management teams, have an obligation to practice intergenerational equity. That is, part of their commitment is to be concerned about the future of the organization. They need to balance what is good for the company now with what will be good in the years and decades ahead. To love an organization means to want it to thrive and continue its life. Boards fall short in their obligation if they hire a chief executive officer who is not concerned with the future beyond his own corporate tenure. They may even encourage short-term executive thinking by rewarding only those leaders who optimize the current financial picture. A maternalistic board bases the CEO's compensation as much on what the leader has done to ensure future success as on the past year's bottom line.

Leaders who love the organization are easily identified by others. They can recognize themselves by answering the following questions:

Leadership Questionnaire #1:
Do You Love the Organization?

1. Do you believe in the organization's mission?

2. Are you passionate in your desire for the organization to succeed?

3. Do your values and those of the organization match?

4. Does your behavior consistently demonstrate a loyalty to the company?

5. Do you make decisions that balance self-love with organizational love? (In other words, are your decisions made with the good of the company in mind?)

6. Do you make decisions that balance what is good for the company today with what is good for the company tomorrow?

If a leader cannot answer yes to all of these questions, the organization and the leader are not a good fit. Organizations can thrive only when their leaders admire them, identify with them, and desire to protect them.

Loving the organization is the first facet of maternalistic management. Alone, it is not enough for leadership, for it could amount to either despotic or martyred bosses. Caring for the company must be balanced with love for the employees, the customers, the community, and the leader. The following chapters address these other parts of maternalism.

$\mathcal{L}$oving the Employee Team

People want to think you care before they care what you think.

— Unknown

An individual organization is different from all others. Its health, culture, mission, goals, values, and personality are as unique as a fingerprint. But organizations do have one thing in common. All are inhabited by people . . . people in departments, people in teams, people as individuals. And people, as we have already established, want to be cared about.

This statement might bring scoffing from some hard-boiled business types who would assert that business is not the place for feelings. They might say this is too feminine a point of view, too soft. "Just like a woman," they might exclaim, "to talk about this mushy, touchy-feely stuff. That's why women don't make good leaders—they're not willing to make the tough decisions or to separate business from personal attachments. Real men (read: real leaders) don't concern themselves with this stuff. Maybe the girls (female workers) need mothering, but men don't need it. Just tell men what to do, give 'em fair pay, and forget about this caring junk."

So men don't need leaders who care; they only want leaders that they can respect. Really? That's not the opinion of at least one traditionally masculine organization, an employer historically known for being "macho," which had this to say in one 1985 publication:

> [They] know if a leader cares and is concerned for their well-being . . . Leaders must not just say they are concerned, they must do things to show concern for their [followers'] well-being: The leader's personal example sets the standard.

This is a quote from a government publication called *Field Manual 22-101.* The parenthesized words are fill-ins for where the manual says "soldiers." The organization is the United States Army.

If the Army understands that men need to feel cared about, this verity should not be difficult for other organizations to accept. All around us is the evidence that people in this society are almost crying out for caring and concern. From childhood to old age, in our personal and our public lives, we humans—male or female—need to feel cared about.

Scientists in the field of human studies have documented that infants who receive adequate food and attention to physical needs, but who receive none of the loving attention we call mothering, suffer and die from marasmus, a wasting away of the body. Without maternalism in the organizations of today, companies too are wasting away. The individuals who people these institutions suffer from a workplace marasmus in which their spirits, talents, and abilities do not develop, even if they are receiving adequate wages and benefits.

Caring for others in a maternal manner does not mean controlling them or "smothering" them. It means helping them—every one of them—develop their own abilities and pursue their own successes.

According to human development expert James Lugo,[1] there are basic differences between what humans perceive as fatherly love and motherly love. He describes fatherly love as conditional; that is, it is withdrawn if it isn't earned. Motherly love has "no strings attached and is considered to be the foundation for all other types of love. It includes feeling responsible for the care and protection of others, and the ability to instill a sense of worth into the loved one."

Self-Esteem

With all the hoopla over self-esteem in the past decade, you'd think that all managers would understand its influence on associates and on the workplace. Certainly loving leaders understand the importance of protecting other people's self-esteem. Parenting books are full of theory on giving children an environment where they will learn to like themselves, and management theory addresses this as well.

Joel Brockner discussed the research and theory of self-esteem in his 1988 book, *Self-esteem at Work.*[2] The following are some of his points:

---

[1] Lugo, J: *Human Development.* New York: Macmillan Publishing Company, 1974.

[2] Brockner, J.: *Self Esteem At Work: Research Theory and Practice.* Lexington, Massachusetts: Lexington Books, 1988.

1. Self-esteem influences an individual's work behaviors and attitude.

2. People have a need to feel good about themselves.

3. Much of what workers do is done to enhance, preserve, and restore self-esteem.

Whenever self-esteem is discussed, the conclusion seems to be that we don't have enough of it. From traumas in childhood to interactions in adulthood, we are faced with experiences that can shake our self-faith and belief in our own worth. Loving leaders are aware of the fragility of human egos, and in their interactions with associates they consciously plan to enhance self-esteem. During discipline, they concentrate their comments on the behavior or actions that need correcting, not on an individual's worth as a person. Maternalistic managers are empathic. Empathic people are authentic, compassionate, and open, which allows them to understand and relate to others in ways that foster human growth, even during discipline. They're concerned with how others feel, are able to put themselves in the other person's place, and want to be fair.

> *Building self-esteem in your child isn't about indiscriminate praise. It's about fostering capability.*
>
> — Jean Illsley Clarke,
> SELF-ESTEEM: A FAMILY AFFAIR

(Building self-esteem in work associates also isn't about indiscriminate praise. It's about fostering capability and work success.)

The basic needs of people don't change with age. Just as a good mother's love is unconditional, so should be a leader's love for others. Some writers have claimed that management is a sacred trust. Bosses control much of the work environment and influence the job satisfaction, mental health, and even physical health of workers. The maternal manager is aware of this and promotes both health and satisfaction. She does this as a mentor, cheerleader, advocate, disciplinarian, ethicist, and futurist. She's a loving leader.

The Mentor

As was mentioned in an earlier chapter, mentoring is often described as the process in which the boss selects a promising subordinate and then takes an active part in helping him with his career. We've accepted this as part of a patriarchal system, but it's not an acceptable mode of operations for the maternalistic leader. Just as a mother would not choose only one of her children to nurture, so would a maternalistic manager not limit his guidance and support to a few, select followers. Loving leadership means mentoring everyone in the organization, by actively thinking about their betterment and taking actions to assist them with their growth. It means making oneself available and paying attention to the opportunities that arise for others. It means contributing whatever one can to helping every single employee be the best they can be. It means encouraging—even pushing —each one to stretch and grow. Sometimes a push from a mentor is the very thing that starts an individual on the road to success.

> *Our chief want in life is somebody who'll make us do what we can.*
>
> — Ralph Waldo Emerson

Common objections to mentoring include: (1) "This is treating people like children. Adults are responsible for their own careers; how presumptuous to believe other people need or even want manager mentoring"; (2) "This is controlling others and making them dependent on the boss for their success"; and (3) "With the large span of control so many managers have today, there's not enough time for leaders to be managing everybody's career." As you will see, none of these objections stands up under examination:

1. Yes, adults are responsible for their own careers, but it is naive to believe that all of us automatically have equal opportunities. Americans who say "It's not what you know, it's who you know" have come to grips with the reality that politics influence career progression. Bosses are at a point in their careers where they have power, position, and political influence. The power inherent to management makes it easier for them to remove roadblocks to the progress of others. Leaders have a responsibility to see the big picture, so they are more aware of opportunities within organizations. Employees have a more narrow vision because they are busy getting their day-to-day jobs done and simply don't have the same time or opportunity that managers have for staying informed. Thus managers have both the power and the information to assist in the career growth of others.

People never outgrow their need for help from other people, and no one—including the boss—got where she did without the assistance and influence of others, whether she recognizes this or not. Managers should give the organizational help that they are in the unique position to provide.

2. Help is not the same thing as control, and the aim of maternalistic management is to encourage others to help themselves, not to carry them to their success. It is not loving to make people dependent on their leader for success (do not mistake the managers who do this for loving leaders). Love includes the encouragement of self-esteem, and a major part of self-esteem is taking responsibility for one's own life. Healthy maternalistic relationships are honest, supportive, and caring. They provide for individual growth by allowing the freedom to be creative and self-directed.

In health care, particularly in the arena of chemical dependency, a condition called codependency is recognized as a block to personal growth. One definition of codependency is that it is an emotional, psychological, and behavioral condition that develops as a result of an individual's prolonged exposure to, and adherence to, a set of oppressive rules. Some rules prevent the open expression of feeling as well as the direct discussion of personal and interpersonal problems. One symptom of codependency is a need to be responsible for other people's needs, thoughts, feelings, actions, and well-being. Modern workplaces, being so full of rules as they are, have fostered a type of codependency between bosses and subordinates that blocks individuals from taking responsibility for their own work lives. This legacy is why wonderfully politically correct management theories like empowerment, decentralized control, or democratic leadership don't always work well. Drastic changes in power and decision-making that occur through changing rules and roles require whole new ways of thinking and acting on both the manager's and employees' parts. Management theories have concentrated on changing the manager's actions, assuming that employees will take to empowerment with joyous competency. They ignore such phenomena as learned helplessness, wherein some people with a history of little or no control become passive and unable to behave assertively. Loving leadership includes the understanding that different individuals require different management at different stages in their career growth. A person's current level of maturity must be considered. The manager's job is to help the associate develop so that he needs progressively less external guidance while gaining self-control. The objective is to provide coaching, education, and opportunities for each person. It is a nurturing that does not foster oppressive dependency.

3. Maternalism does not mean micromanaging every subordinate's career. Depending on the span of control, type of industry, organizational culture, and individual abilities, it can include general organizational policies that encourage growth through education, risk-taking, and job enlargement, or more individualized career counseling, or both. When a manager says, "I don't have time to concern myself with my employees' success," he's sending two very distinct messages. The first is that he cares little for the individuals with whom he works; the second is that he doesn't care about the

organization that has employed him as a boss. If he does care about the company's well-being, and if he understands how important his own role is to the success of individuals and the company itself, he will certainly want the employees to be the best that they can be.

As was stated above, a leader's management position gives him an opportunity to help others succeed, through both his influence on policies and procedures and his access to information about opportunities. His conscious concern for the well-being of others will enable him to give advice and make decisions and recommendations that can contribute heavily to their success.

Helping others succeed means helping the organization succeed. If a company is to excel, it requires quality, dedicated, well-trained, enthusiastic employees. Where are go-getters of this type likely to be found: in the organization where they feel uncared for, unchallenged, and stagnant, or in the institution where they are appreciated, challenged, and encouraged to be all that they can be? Time and time again it has been shown that increasing an individual's responsibility can be beneficial to the company as much as to the worker. Managers are mostly hired to manage "human resources," and what better "husbandry" (good, careful management) of these resources than to increase their value to the organization by nurturing them for growth?

The Cheerleader

When Jonathan Sanford played his first Little League baseball game, his team was thoroughly defeated. His mother thought he might be upset by the one-sided victory, so she will never forget his post-game words: "Mommy, that was great. It was so much more fun than I thought, because people watched and cheered for me." He seemed oblivious to winning or losing; what excited him were the yells of encouragement from the audience. They motivated him to play his very best.

Adults are motivated by the same thing. We want to be cheered by others when we're winning . . . and also when we're trying to play the game, even if we're not as successful as we'd like to be.

Loving leaders cheer their associates on. They are generous with words of encouragement. They appreciate the skills, talents, and contribution of every individual and of the team as a whole. But they don't just give words of approval themselves. They nurture a culture where they serve as chief cheerleaders, leading others to applaud and acclaim their co-workers and themselves. They don't give their positive feedback in a whisper, or keep it behind closed doors. Cheerleaders aren't shy with their praise—they shout their approval and congratulations. Cheerleading managers, too, inspire others by supporting them publicly.

Cheerleading not only praises a job well done, but also gives support when the result is not a win. Cheerleaders aren't fair weather friends—they're out there yelling and inspiring their teams to do their very best even when they're losing the game. Maternal environments are places where associates feel safe taking risks because they know their leader's approval won't be withdrawn because of a loss.

Loving leaders give others unconditional positive regard.

That is, they care about the self-worth of others and they appreciate them as people, win or lose. They understand that their associates will not try new things or consider new ideas if they are rewarded only when they succeed.

One more thing: cheerleading happens in a place of cheer, as in joy and happiness. A workplace without cheer is rightly called cheerless. Who wants to work in a cheerless, depressing place?

Loving Leaders as Cheerleaders

My boss was the inspiration I needed to go back to college part-time and finish my degree. She arranged the schedule to help me, and then, when I graduated, she had the company throw a party for all of us who'd completed higher education, complete with a speech from the CEO and recognition of our families!

(That's cheerleading!)

I love working at this place. Whenever I accomplish something, the manager I work for not only notices it, but tells me thanks.

(That's cheerleading!)

The best part of my yearly evaluation is reading about specific stuff I've done well. My boss doesn't just write that I'm a good salesman. He writes about the Martin account or how I handled a particular unhappy customer. It feels good to know he's aware of me and my job.

(That's cheerleading!)

Whenever I'm feeling unsuccessful I just pull out my file of "attaboys" to remind myself that I've done some really great stuff. They're just little hand-written notes my boss sends me that say I'm appreciated for certain projects or hard work. I've even got notes from her about things I've done for the community, like Girl Scouts volunteer work, saying how proud it makes her to be associated with me.

(That's cheerleading!)

Last year I convinced my manger that we needed to change the check-off procedure between two of our departments. She said I was the expert and to go ahead. Well, we tried the change and it didn't work, so we had to go back to the old way. I could have felt like a failure, but you know what she said? She thanked me for caring about the company and trying to improve things. She said I had courage to try changes and then to be willing to change back when I realized it didn't work the way I'd thought.

(That's cheerleading!)

Cheering leaders bolster confidence. Their support shows that they are paying attention to others' strivings. While some managers actively criticize and place barriers in associates' paths rather than support them, a larger number provide disincentives to motivation by simply being oblivious to others' hard work and successes. They seem to ignore people as long as operations are "running OK," and only give feedback when there's a problem. Their inattentiveness is more demoralizing

> *Workers have all this incredible communications technology at their disposal, but often what people really want is two minutes face-to-face with a boss or co-worker.*
>
> – Chuck Darrah, Anthropology Department Chair,
> San Jose State University, quoted by
> Tom McNichol in USA WEEKEND

than the over-control of a micromanager. Love means paying attention, and cheerleading is the most positive form of attention.

Remember that paying attention requires being there for others. The need for "face time" between supervisors and associates cannot be underestimated. Just as parenting can't be done long distance, management is one job that cannot be done without personal interaction.

The Advocate

Advocacy is the active support of something, and the advocate is a person who supports, defends and "goes to bat" for a thing he values. There are advocates for the environment, for certain laws, for special interest groups, for anything and everything you can think of. Life is complex, with interests and demands pulling in so many directions that, without advocates, the success of any idea or group would be unlikely.

Work organizations are complex, too. Even within a company with a clear mission and goals, there are a variety of organizational needs that are sometimes not complementary. There are counterbalancing needs for resources, income, and quality, as well as for personal and departmental success. No matter how independent a work team, how democratic a leader, how empowered the associated individuals, projects and everyday work won't get done without advocates. And the most powerful advocate is the formal leader, the boss.

The maternalistic leader serves as an advocate by championing the associates' needs and ideas. She ensures that resources are available so that jobs can get done. She provides education and training when it's needed. She helps others by giving them what they need to help themselves. She is of service to the people who work for the company in the way that a good mother is of service to her children.

Being of service to associates is a central premise of many modern management theories. Future workplaces are foreseen as organizations where those who actually perform front-line work are able to plan, organize, and control their own work activities. Managers will be coordinators, not leaders. Whatever they are called, they'll be needed as advocates for their work groups. Managers are the ones who have the time and know-how to navigate the political mine fields of complex organizations. They support by cutting through bureaucratic red tape, managing conflict within and outside of the work groups, and providing an environment where workers have the time and training to plan, organize, and control their own work within the overall mission and direction of the company.

Leaders as advocates spread the word about their associates. They brag about others' accomplishments. They let other departments, other leaders, and the community know about team and individual success. They understand the psychology of self-esteem, and how important praise, recognition, and interpersonal communications are to its maintenance. They understand that work stress is not caused by hard work but by a lack of control over work, and they advocate giving control to those who do the work. They have a good grasp on the reality of who really makes an organization successful: the people who perform the core work, supported by advocate leaders.

Advocate managers realize something else, too: that the customer isn't always right. In today's atmosphere of consumerism and customer satisfaction movements, it may seem heretical to assert that customers are sometimes wrong. Every business journal seems to include an article on the importance of treating well the purchasers of our products and services. Managers know very well that each employee represents the company, and that a consumer's interactions with a single employee may determine whether he will continue to patronize the business. But wise managers also know that a customer may have unrealistic expectations. For example, the hospital "customer" (otherwise known as a patient) who is receiving medication after surgery may believe that he should be pain-free. In reality, there is usually postoperative discomfort even with the use of narcotics. Blaming the nurse because he hurts is an example of customer anger caused by inaccurate perceptions. The customer expectation that a service or product will provide instant gratification or even change one's life is sure to result in dissatisfaction.

Some clients or customers may be people who habitually abuse others; others will take out their frustrations by being rude or demeaning to those trying to serve them. Every service employee can recall times when, no matter how polite or accommodating the employee tried to be, she or he was rewarded with verbal abuse. Because the advocate leader realizes customers aren't always right, he doesn't expect associates to be doormats to customers or to accept verbal or physical abuse in their jobs. As their advocate, he makes sure they have training in how to act when customers are abusive or impossible to please. He stands up for his associates (respectfully, of course)—even to the customer. He knows how to be an advocate while still practicing good customer relations.

Advocate managers also champion their employees' right to be fully developed human beings, not simple automatons invented and existing for the benefit of the company eight, ten, twelve, or more hours a day. They understand that working people have personal lives, and that the home life is important. They recognize the inevitability of conflicts between work and home life, and are willing to handle them with respect and flexibility. They advocate company policies that will help workers achieve balanced lives. These policies might include concepts like job sharing, part-time jobs, flexible work hours, company help with child care and elder care, classes in parenting and stress management, and time off for doctor appointments and school activities.

> *Valuing people and respecting their need to balance home and work life will demonstrate the respect for each individual's inherent dignity.*
>
> — Karlene Kerfoot, Executive Vice President

How to Be an Advocate and
Still Practice Good Customer Relations

1. Give customer-relations training to all of your service associates. Besides teaching the usual courtesy and public relations, train people in how to act when the customer is abusive or impossible to please.

2. Expect your associates to be courteous. Hold them accountable for good customer relations, and include their customer-relations skills in evaluations. But also be lavish with praise when an associate demonstrates skill at dealing with the difficult customer.

3. Don't expect your associates to be "doormats" to the customer. No one should have to take verbal or physical abuse in her job. Well-trained employees should know how to react with dignity and courtesy but without accepting personal attacks.

4. Listen to the associate's side of the story before deciding what to do in response to a customer complaint.

5. When an apology to a customer is called for, don't make derogatory comments about employees. "I'm sorry this occurred; I will correct this matter," is appropriate. Saying, "This was caused by that stupid clerk; he'll be fired," is not.

6. Be sure that associates know how you respond to customer complaints and why. Even when the customer is not right, it is sometimes appropriate for a manager to use "smoothing" techniques that might appear to the uninformed as a lack of support for the employee.

7. Turn customer-service problems into growth-and-learning opportunities for associates. Sharing experiences will help reinforce customer-relations training.

Thoughts on Balancing the Working Life
With the Personal Life

Managers Define Hero Role Model: Bosses Found to Win Loyalty With Sensitivity to Employees' Work-Life Conflicts

> – Headline, NEWS TRIBUNE, Tacoma, Washington, 5/9/96

As a manager, you are renting a worker's behavior, not buying his or her soul. It's a problem when bosses expect people to work overtime, take work home at night, forego family and personal interests, have work be the center of their lives . . . most people leave the office wanting to be free to enjoy their family, friends, and activities.

> – Bruce Hyland and Merle Yost, HEMISPHERE

The mission statement of Levi Strauss is maternalistic in that it says the company wants "an environment supportive of employees balancing their work and personal lives, involving all aspects of life," not just child care or elder care.

Flexible work arrangements positively affect retention, have a beneficial impact on recruitment, create higher productivity, and have a positive effect on morale.

> – Research results of studies done by
> the national organization Catalyst

Enter the New Hero: A Boss Who Knows You Have a Life

> – Headline, THE WALL STREET JOURNAL, 5/9/96

The Disciplinarian

Because it is accepted that children need guidance in order to grow into responsible members of society, parenting theories always include ideas about how to discipline. But modern management theories are less likely to remember the importance of discipline for adults. In fact, there seems to be a general distaste for the very idea that an associate would ever need something so demeaning as a reprimand. According to this line of thinking, "People are basically good and want to do a good job. If allowed to do so, they will do their jobs in the best way for the company and the customer. Self-governing workers don't need bosses to tell them what to do."

True, most people want to do good work. But there are some who, because of family background, societal conditioning, or placement in a job that isn't right for them, don't have the drive to provide superior performance. They're willing to let others carry the ball, do the work, and worry about the organization's success. Even those who want to be superior performers can sometimes flounder and mess up. Skillfully applied discipline can help these individuals grow into responsible members of the organization.

Discipline means the taking of certain actions to train others by correcting them. Parenting specialists disagree on types and methods of discipline, but the majority come to the same conclusion: Loving parents must discipline. It is a demonstration of their love that they care enough to enforce rules for their children's safe growth on their journey to adulthood.

Loving leaders discipline, too. They have a responsibility to the organization, its customers, the work force in aggregate,

> *A context of caring comes first, confrontation follows. A context of caring can be created when a person is truly for another, genuinely concerned about another, authentically related to another. The context of such caring is, however, not a blank check approval of the other. The core of true caring is a clear invitation to grow, to become what he or she truly is and can be, to move toward maturity.*
>
> – David Augsburger, CARING ENOUGH TO CONFRONT

and the individual associate to be sure that standards are set in the organization and that people are held accountable to those standards. When standards of work performance or organizational behavior are not met, it's up to the manager to reprimand. This can mean anything from having a conversation about work areas needing improvement to verbal and written warnings about the consequences of not improving to actual job termination.

Reprimanding employees isn't a pleasure. For most bosses, it's one of the most difficult parts of the job. The most successful business person, who may be able to analyze situations, solve complex problems, and negotiate successful contracts, can become an unsure, incompetent, reluctant, stammering manager when forced to confront an employee with corrective action. Bosses are poorly prepared to criticize other people, and the result is that some will yell, demean, and verbally abuse, while others will refuse to confront because they want to avoid unpleasantness. Maternalistic leaders recognize the need to discipline and have learned how to do it.

Love includes caring enough to confront. Without confronting problems and providing discipline where it is called for, a leader can destroy an organization's morale, causing decreasing productivity and loss of business. The leader who thinks she is being kind when she chooses not to discipline (just like the parent who chooses not to discipline) is actually doing a disservice to the undisciplined individual. Human growth is furthered by trust, and true trust is possible only when there is openness and feedback.

The most unkind, unloving leadership act of all is to avoid the responsibility of helping others to grow because of one's own immaturity in dealing with problems. Appropriate discipline, correctly delivered, is essential to an individual's long-term success. To be appropriate and loving, the discipline must be applied with the underlying goal of helping the individual and the organization succeed. It should be delivered in a timely manner—soon after whatever event precipitated the discipline need. It should be delivered in a sensitive manner, which usually means privately.

Discipline must be based on standards that are evenly applied across the organization. In order to be effective, it requires consistency. The best parents and the best managers are consistent; their children and their associates know what to expect from them. They make as few rules as possible, and then hold everyone in the family or company to the same rules. The loving leader gives feedback for the sake of others' growth and for the good of the company, not to meet her own needs for power or control.

Corrective action can only correct when it is perceived to be fair. In Chapter One, fairness is listed as the number-one characteristic thought by employees to exemplify the best bosses. Adults, like children, have a need to perceive an even-handedness in their treatment. In America we place a high value on fair play and equality, and nothing can undermine a workplace morale faster than the perception that the boss has favorites, or isn't fair. When the author was a child, she would sometimes protest to her father when she thought that something was unfair, either to her or to someone else. His answer was uniformly, "Well, the world isn't fair." She grew up with a conviction that is essential to maternalistic management: *True, the world may not be consistently fair, but each of us should be committed to make whatever we can influence more fair!*

A company environment is widely perceived to be fair when:

+ Decisions are consistent with rules.

+ Policies and rules are based on explainable and explained logic or ethics.

+ Policies and rules are impartially enforced for all, regardless of race, sex, age, religion, family connections, personal friendships, or personal lifestyles.

+ Promotion is available to all associates based on ability, regardless of race, sex, age, religion, family connections, personal friendships, or personal lifestyles.

+ Every associate has an opportunity to be mentored.

+ Discipline is free of favoritism or bias.

+ Flexibility is practiced in bending rules for exceptional circumstances.

+ Such flexibility is available to everyone equally.

+ The rationale for bending rules is communicated.

Discipline is usually progressive, in that it becomes more severe if corrective action doesn't work. The ultimate disciplinary action is firing an employee. This may not seem very maternal: mothers don't fire their children, do they? Well, yes, sometimes they do, and we call it tough love, or "kicking the kid out of the nest." There are times when loving leaders have to terminate the relationship between the company and an associate because he can't be helped, can't be improved, and can't be trained for his particular job or company. Maternalism means love for the company and all of the employees, and sometimes it is for the good of the company and the co-workers that an individual must leave. Sometimes firing is the only ethical option.

The Ethicist

A few years ago some schools of business came up with a radical idea. They proposed adding courses in ethics to their curricula. They had identified a need for business ethics, specifically, to be taught to future organization leaders. Some proclaimed this was needed in an unethical society. Ethical behavior had to be taught in college courses because people hadn't learned it in their formative years. Many were pleased with the new classes, expressing satisfaction that the importance of ethical behavior was being recognized, even in a world where many live by the rule "All's fair in love, war, and business."

Ethics are principles of right, moral, or good conduct. The American heritage includes high standards for duty, honesty, and morality, and despite current thought that these are no longer a widespread part of our culture, mainstream Americans still believe, and even long for, their inclusion in our personal, political, and business lives. It is widely suspected, though, that Big Business suffers from Ethics Deficiency Disease (see Chapter Three).

Just what does Ethics Deficiency Disease (EDD) look like? The misuse of in-vogue management theories for a leader's own career purposes is a classic example of EDD. Accusing associates of not being team players simply because they don't agree with the boss is another. If the company is professing to value teamwork, such an accusation can neutralize others' ideas by placing them in a defensive position. Equally unethical is claiming to have participatory management and then cynically manipulating employees by withholding information, allowing participation only in inconsequential decisions, or pretending that a decision was made by staff members when it was actually a management dictum. (This is called pseudoparticipatory management.)

Loving the employee team includes giving them ethical leadership. Ethical leaders are role models because they set high personal standards for themselves and for their associates. They do everything they can to assist others to meet those standards. (Sometimes they do this by simply getting out of the way so that other people can do their jobs.)

Leadership ethics includes treating all associates equitably, without prejudice, harassment, or discrimination of any kind. Ethical behavior means integrity and honesty in bad times as well as good.

One management thought has been that employees should be told good news but spared the pain of hearing the bad stuff. According to this thinking, followers need to see the boss as upbeat and optimistic, even in times of company crisis. This theory is reminiscent of the big debate in hospital care twenty-five years ago, on whether or not to tell a patient he was dying. In those days (not all that long ago), some healthcare professionals actually believed that people didn't have the right to know everything about their own body and life. Not only were those caregivers presumptive about their superior medical knowledge, but they were foolish enough to pretend that patients didn't have the sense to know their lives were near the end. Fortunately, it is now widely known that patients have the right and the need to know their prognoses, so that they can better participate in fighting their illness and can make plans for themselves and their loved ones.

Parenting theory has developed along the same lines. At one time, experts claimed that parents should not burden their children with anything unpleasant. Death, family illness, and money problems were kept secret from the kids. Modern thought is that strong, well-adjusted people come from families with open, shared communication about both "good" and "bad" stuff. Of course, how communication is accomplished and shared depends on the age and maturity of the children.

In this area, managers' ideas haven't evolved as quickly as medical or parenting thinking. Most managers still seem to assume that employee maturity isn't advanced enough to deal with unpleasant news, or they fear that bad news might affect the morale of the work force and cause a drop in productivity. The epitome of this kind of thinking is shown when an organization is in decline. As the bottom line edges further into the red, the boss may exhort people to work harder, without explaining why. She may believe that the workers couldn't handle the bad news or that they wouldn't understand the high finance, or she may fear that her best workers might jump ship if they knew the barge was sinking. So she doesn't share the information, and may even indulge in cheerful little white lies about how well things are going. The result is that intuitive, sharp-eyed employees see through her (and may start looking for other jobs anyway), while the associates who could help turn things around keep right on doing their work in the usual manner, unaware that they should and could be working with management to solve problems and save the company. When the day of reckoning comes, many of those who receive their pink slips are shocked and unprepared.

Honesty, then, is a principal tenet of leadership ethics. It includes the sharing of bad news as well as good. Honesty is demonstrated by leaders who can admit their own mistakes and apologize for errors. It is not censorship of the truth, nor is it white lies to protect the work force. Honesty is essential to maternalism, because people require truthful information in order to grow and become the best individuals that they can be.

Ethical leaders . . .

> . . . communicate openly and honestly, in a straightforward manner.

> . . . admit mistakes, failures, and imperfections (in themselves and in the company).

> . . . apologize when apology is appropriate.

> . . . treat all associates equally.

> . . . consider associates' welfare both today and tomorrow when making decisions.

> . . . set high standards for themselves.

> . . . examine their own actions and evaluate them for moral content.

They do not . . .

> . . . take credit for the work of others.

> . . . ask an associate to lie or to behave in an unethical manner.

> . . . practice sexism, racism, or harassment.

In healthcare institutions, ethical questions come up in life-and-death decisions regarding patients. In certain businesses, ethics are involved in questions of ecology, competition, and product development. These may be seen as difficult gray areas because of benefits and harmful effects that may result from the same decision. Some companies have actually set up ethics departments to help leaders and associates figure out what is ethical behavior. Leadership ethics, or how bosses interact with associates, may not even be considered by these ethicists, yet leadership ethics are not difficult to sort into ethical and unethical behaviors. It's another case of "We know 'em when we see 'em."

Ethical, honest leadership includes direct, truthful communication. It includes courtesy, kindness, and empathy. It includes self-evaluation by leaders, the maturity to admit mistakes, and the grace to apologize when apologies are appropriate. It is not about saving face or appearing perfect. It is about moral behavior and true consideration of associates' present and future well-being.

The Futurist

Caring about the future of one's associates requires a projection of what the future holds for the company and the individual employees.

These days, some of the most profitable consulting businesses appear to be in the field of futurism. Bold prognosticators, studying present indications, predict the world of two, ten, fifteen, twenty, or one hundred years from today. Companies and industries listen to these prophecies in the hope that, by gleaning an insight into the days and years to come, they can make appropriate profit-maximizing decisions. While some futurists compare themselves to fortune tellers of old, smilingly referring to their views of tomorrow as pictures in their crystal balls, most are not at all similar to mystical palm readers or tarot practitioners. The professional futurists who write books or give speeches on the coming changes in the world have a more practical basis for their predictions, such as today's trends or scientific and technological expectations. They study, they read, and they keep their eyes open to everything around them, continually asking, "How will this development alter the future? How will this new fact of today influence tomorrow?"

Maternalistic leaders are futurists, too. In today's world of rapid change, they have to be. Part of loving an employee team is keeping the business alive so that the employees will have jobs, and that means anticipating the future and adjusting for survival.

It can be argued that everyone in business should read and should observe the world around them, because personal survival demands the ability to adjust to future trends. This is true; individuals are responsible for their own lives. But in reality it is an organization's leaders who are more likely to get the information needed for forecasting. The boss's crystal ball, murky as it may be, is probably clearer than that of the front-line worker. Workers are busy getting the work of the business done. Leaders have more access to the numbers, statistics, industry trends, and intercompany small talk. On the other hand, the most lucent crystal balls belong to leaders who listen to input and ideas from the front lines. It takes information from within as well as without to chart a course for organizational adaptation to a changing world.

Why is futurism essential to a company? Because accurate or fairly accurate predictions help the company avoid crises, because futuristic companies can ensure that they're going to be relevant by meeting customers' future needs, and because with knowledge of future trends the company and

> Leaders are responsible for what happens in the future.
>
> — Max DePree, retired CEO of Herman-Miller

> [Most companies are so poor at managing for the future that] "60 to 70 percent of companies don't have good succession plans below the CEO."
>
> — Robert Lefton, CEO, Psychological Associates

> But some leaders are helping others get ready for the future, like the president of United Technologies, who according to BUSINESS WEEK, 2/26/94, has "invented a nifty program to help workers re-educate themselves for their next jobs."

the employees can make appropriate preparations for thriving, not just surviving.

Any historian can illustrate the dangers of not practicing futurism. Of the one hundred largest United States companies in 1900, only sixteen still exist. In the 1980s, two hundred thirty companies (46 percent) slipped out of the Fortune 500. Somehow, they had not adapted to a changing world. Either they did not have talented company futurists or they chose to disregard them. In spite of the advantages of leadership futurism, many companies still don't respect or reward their internal futurists. This may be because the company's highest leadership is blinded by its past successes and is unable to conceive of current practices not being successful tomorrow. It may be because futurists talk about change, which may be seen as bad news. They get reputations as being negative, rather than positive optimists cheering about how great things are today. Sometimes futurism isn't important to top executives because leaders see themselves as temporary in a company—needing to make a spectacular splash of success today, even at the cost of the organization's future. They can move on to another temporary prestigious job with another organization. And sometimes companies fail to respect futurists because crisis management has become the norm for leaders.

Managing from crisis to crisis can be addictive because handling emergent situations is stimulating. Crises make heroes of the leaders who successfully weather them. In fact, often the managers who are admired by their superiors and promoted are those who have been able to showcase their talents by solving dramatic problems. Less successful at climbing corporate ladders are the futuristic leaders, who appear never even to have difficulties in their departments. Because they manage proactively, they're able to make changes that solve potential problems before they even occur. Some theorists claim that this is a female approach, and one that contributes to the glass ceiling because it is unseen, unacknowledged, and unrewarded.

Whether or not futuristic leadership is a female approach, it is a maternalistic approach, because it insulates the company and the company's people from trauma. Avoidance of crises saves stress, money, and individual jobs. Who knows how many layoffs and job losses could have been avoided in the last decade if leaders had made it a goal to plan for the organization's future, in order to save employment opportunities?

Of course, even the most futuristic leader is unable to predict everything. Some crises will occur, for no one has a perfectly clear crystal ball. But the leader who tries to understand the future and its effects on the organization and on individuals within the organization will greatly reduce the pain that comes with change in slushy times.

Some major changes occurring right now result from a shift in the kind of work Americans do. Many jobs have been lost as the United States has moved from manufacturing to an information-dominated economy. Even service companies, such as airlines and hospitals, are now facing upheavals for which few were prepared. Yet futurists have been predicting these very developments for years.

It is now being predicted that the days of staying with one company or one profession or one type of career for an entire work life are gone. People, it is said, will spend much of their adult life in school, training for their next career. There will be no loyalty to a particular company because workers of tomorrow, like many executives of today, will be "just passing through." As work requirements change, current "obsolete" workers will be let go and replaced with new workers who have the needed new skills.

This vision of tomorrow is based on the rapid changes in technology to which we are just beginning to grow accustomed. It does not take into account the needs that people have to belong and be cared about.

> In the era of downsizing and layoffs and an
> increasing reliance on lower-cost temporary
> help, American corporations feel much less
> like home than they did a generation ago. . . .
> So if—at the same time that Americans are
> depending on the workplace for the funda-
> mental warmth and reassurance of human
> contact—the understanding going in is that a
> job can, and probably will, end at any time,
> there may be trouble ahead.
>
> — Bob Greene, syndicated columnist,
> NEWS TRIBUNE, Tacoma, Washington, 9/1/97

Since the future can be what we make of it, maternalistic companies won't accept a future devoid of concern for employees. They will plan for the future, determine how the company must adapt, determine what skills future employees will need, and provide the training today for the jobs of tomorrow. In other words, they won't throw out the old employees to make room for the new ones; to the extent possible, they'll provide ways to retool the old to meet new challenges. Even though job-hopping and career-hopping are expected to become the norm, these organizations will be willing to give associates the constant training and retraining needed for success in their company or in other companies to which the workers may have to move.

Within the healthcare industry, recent events in the nursing profession provide an excellent example of how maternalistic leaders can influence the future of others. Hospitals have long been the standard workplace for registered nurses; in fact, in the past the majority of nurses have spent their entire careers in hospitals. With new pressure to control costs, and the advent of more outpatient and home-treatment possibilities, hospitals are experiencing a decreasing inpatient population. It is projected that, within a few years, the majority of nursing jobs will be outside the hospital. The new jobs will require a higher level of education for those who want to practice professional nursing.

Nursing had been considered a safe career. It was said, "If you're a nurse, you can always get a job." But now angry, bewildered nurses are being laid off, and are having trouble finding new jobs. Futurists have predicted these changes for several years, yet the nurses were taken by surprise. They weren't included in the administrative meetings where these developments were foretold; they didn't hear consultants warning their executives. And apparently they didn't have maternalistic, futuristic leaders.

Maternalistic leaders, as futurists, would have made it their business to watch the trends, prognosticate, and share their prognostications with associates. They would have given career counseling, not as dictums but as opinions. They would have taken steps to help their entire team prepare for change, by:

+ Sharing facts and predictions

+ Giving opinions and hearing associates' opinions about what those facts and predictions portended for the profession, the institution, and individual careers

+ Providing training on change theory

+ Providing training for new jobs.

Sometimes facing change is unpleasant; no one likes to hear that the job they do so well today may be obsolete tomorrow. Many leaders avoid talking about the future because they themselves don't want to think about it or they want to avoid associates' anger or other strong emotions. They may tell themselves that they're not responsible for what the future brings, that it is paternalistic and disempowering to interfere with associates' careers because—after all—every individual is responsible for her own career. Maternalistic leaders, in contrast, couldn't sleep well at night without taking concerned action—not to control associates and not to disempower them, but to share information that might help them to make decisions. They would share whatever they knew or believed, because they might have a clearer crystal ball than others, and what they shared might be just what was necessary for individuals to take control and retool their own careers.

That's maternalism. That's futurism. That's caring for others. It's one of the traits that distinguishes the mediocre boss from the leader.

The Leader

Many of today's management theorists are talking about the need to become stewards rather than leaders, to facilitate groups rather than manage them. These are intuitively appealing theories because of the bosses' poor reputations, and because much of what has passed for leadership in the

> *Many working people aren't suited to the empowerment system. They balk at the subtle control mechanisms often used. They simply want to put in their eight hours and be done with it.*
>
> — Timothy Appel, THE WALL STREET JOURNAL, 9/8/97

past has been practiced by egocentric, autocratic bullies or kindly but patronizing father figures.

The problem with these new theories is that they: (1) assume that people who have never had power and its requisite responsibility will jump at the chance to be in control and will know how to lead themselves, (2) forget that there are widely divergent ways of looking at the work, so that coordinated groups or teams of disagreeing workers may be unable to make progress without leaders, and (3) underestimate the difficulty individuals have in considering the company's needs to be as important as their own (what's best for an individual is not always what's best for the group or organization).

Some management practitioners have taken democratic theories to heart to such an extent that their organizations flounder while consensus is sought on every detail. A middle manager in the aerospace industry recently complained, "Our management team has become a bunch of sheep . . . with no shepherd. We want to be good managers so we bring in consultants to tell us the latest good-manager stuff. The latest stuff talks about being coordinators, so we've thrown leadership out. Everyone is supposed to be equally 'empowered.' If you don't espouse the new theories, you're labeled as 'stuck in an old paradigm' and 'not a team player.' "

That last charge is an effective jibe for today. Everyone wants to be seen as a team player, because if you're branded as being otherwise, you're a bad employee. *After all,* this thinking goes, *team players are working together for the good of the whole company, so if you choose not to be part of the team, you're not working for the company's best interests.* In reality, teamwork is much more difficult than most people assume. Even if a group of people is comprised of individuals who all want to do the right thing for the organization, those group members will have unique ideas about what is right and how to do it. The best team members are those who are willing to listen to others' views and then present their own ideas for open discussion and problem solving. Unfortunately, the term "teamwork" is now all too often being used to manipulate people into subservience or lock-step compliance: if you don't agree with someone in power, you're not a team player.

> *What gets me is that my values obviously don't match the big guys'. I was brought up to believe you don't steal. I still get shocked when I read about administrators who rip off their institutions. Did you know that from 1985 to 1996 there were at least one hundred executives indicted for stealing $38 million from their own hospitals? What do you bet that no one caught them earlier because anyone who questioned their actions was nailed for not being a team player?*
>
> – A hospital nursing director

*It's all politics. Someone comes up with a really
Bozo idea, and everybody says "Wow, great idea"
. . . then a brave soul tells it like it really is, and says,
"Have you thought about this?" or "There might be
a better way." Bam! No matter how nice he says it,
he's in trouble with the powers that be because
he's not a team player.*

— A sergeant in the United States Army

*Corporate life is a sham. It pretends to use all
these values: partnership, teamwork . . . and all
the while you're being lied to by the smiling guys
in pinstriped suits.*

— A Wall Street specialist, quoted in NEWSWEEK

That the type of leadership demonstrated by an organization's managers strongly affects the morale and productivity
of an organization is usually not disputed. It is generally
known that nit-picky, micromanaging bosses who try to control everybody and everything can cause subordinate burnout. So can managers who are condescending or emotionally
out of control or just plain mean. But equally damaging to
the company is the nonleader in a leadership position, because a lack of leadership destroys morale just as much as
micromanaging does.

In the past, nonleadership was labeled as "laissez-faire
management": leave them alone and they (the workers) will
work out the best way to do their jobs. This school of management thinking ignored, as do some of today's ideas, the
principle of learned helplessness. This conditioned worker

helplessness must be unlearned before we jump in to the true sharing of ownership and responsibility for a company, throughout the company. As the progeny of a paternalistic society, we have too long been taught that we are helpless pawns—workers dependent on managers who take responsibility. This conditioning has fostered narrow viewpoints and the need to have decisions made by someone else so that accountability can be avoided. It would be hard enough to unlearn this learned helplessness in places of employment, but its magnitude as a societal behavior makes the unlearning a formidable task. If the goal is to instantaneously create a work force of associates who can assert authority and also accept the accountability currently falling to managers, then our culture has set us up for failure. We may want authority —yes—but accountability? No!

Compounding the problem of moving from centralized, paternalistic leadership to truly shared organizational leadership is the hyperspeed change in all areas of modern life, the amount of information available, and the lack of stable employment projected to be upcoming. More information has become available to humans in the last thirty years than during the previous five thousand—and each organization needs as much of it as possible. Getting information to all those who need it is a major challenge for modern organizations.

Shared organizational leadership assumes that every worker will not only want to do the best possible job, but will make decisions based on what's best for the company. At the same time that we push this theory, we're also projecting the idea (discussed earlier in this book) that we're

Accountability in American Society:
Examples of Our Aversion

"Someday my prince will come..."

> – Snow White, the princess who waited to be saved
> by a knight in shining armor, rather than take
> accountability for her own destiny

"Without you, I am nothing...nothing at all."

> – Sentiment of the majority of popular love songs,
> implying that our happiness and self-esteem
> depend on someone else, not ourselves

"He should not be treated too harshly in our criminal justice system, because he himself is a victim of..." (abuse, society, racism, poverty, circumstances — you name it). The idea is that adults aren't responsible for their own crimes (even murder) because, after all, 96 percent of us come from dysfunctional families.

"That's what you get paid the big bucks for."

> – The oft-heard refrain of workers who want
> to hand back decision-making and account-
> ability to the managers who have "thrust"
> these company problems upon them

"Accountability is one of today's most popular buzz-words. Yet in my work as a management consultant I am frequently struck by how quickly people at all levels abdicate responsibility and blame others for their problems."

> – Dr. Nathaniel Brandon, clinical psychologist,
> quoted in BOTTOM LINE PERSONAL

entering an era of transient employer-employee relationships. We're talking about the idea of steady jobs being replaced by people who belong to a contingency work force. Job security is considered something out of history, and company-worker loyalty is to be replaced by contractual obligations between part-time, temporary, just-passing-through employees and organizations.

In this world of no attachments, how do you empower employees to make decisions for an organization to which they owe nothing? If they feel they don't matter, that they're just temps passing through, how familiar will they be with the company's mission or goals? How committed will they be to making decisions for the good of the company?

Many bosses don't look at the dichotomy between the coexisting trends of empowerment and the temporary work force. They also don't consider the huge leap from paternalism to empowerment, which seems to call for an interim management style that provides the tools necessary to take on authority, responsibility, and accountability. They abdicate leadership by bringing in consultants and accepting new theories that become the management bible of the organization. They accept employee empowerment as a way to rid themselves of carrying all the responsibility. As observed by the aerospace industry manager, they become sheep. Rather than leading, they are led by a theory or a theorist. Sometimes they latch on to one favorite piece of theory and use it to justify their own behaviors.

Leadership requires clear thinking. While staying educated about theory and change, loving leaders continue to think for themselves. They consider the circumstances of their own company, society, and associates, and they continue to be leaders. Anything less than this is management malpractice.

Comments on Nonleader Leaders

We brought in this management guru last year and sent all of our management team to a three-day retreat with him. We bought his book for everybody who attended. He didn't really have any new commandments. Now, whatever decision is made, you hear, "Well, this is how 'B' [the consultant] said we should do it." The worst thing is that some people take little pieces of what he said and use that as a weapon. You know: if I don't agree with what someone says, he says, "Well, I'm just doing what we learned from 'B'"... and that's taken as justification for anything.

— A middle manager

We're such a bureaucratic company — too slow to take action, and with too many layers of management. By the time we get done analyzing and agonizing over every decision, our competitors have gobbled up every new line of business. It's like all the change going on has frozen our CEO. He says he's a Tom Peters fan, and Tom Peters wrote one column that said it may be the best thing to do NOTHING in chaotic times. So that's what we're doing, while the bottom line sinks slowly into the pink.

— A company vice president

> I think our company is way behind in the quality-
> assurance movement. We've been arguing for
> eighteen months over whether we're going to
> follow the "Deming model" or the "Juran way."
> There's even some diehard Crosby fans. I say it's
> the concept of improving our services that's
> important, not slavish adherence to some model.
> Why can't we just agree on the concept and set
> up our own way? Something that works for us.
> Oh yeah, I forgot, none of us is smart enough for
> that . . . we've got to be told what to do by some
> expensive consultant."
>
> — A first-line manager

Management malpractice, like medical malpractice, can be either improper or negligent practices or treatment of others. Improper management includes the rude, cruel, unloving, autocratic, esteem-destroying, disempowering behaviors that the popular media associate with the word "boss." (We try to find humor about this type of leader in books like Rod Zolkos's *Bosses and Other Reptiles*.) Just as lethal to workers, though perhaps not as well diagnosed, is negligent leadership. And negligent leadership may be on the rise, as managers use new empowerment theories as a rationale to abandon the responsibility of management.

In health care, malpractice can lead to something called iatrogenic illness, which means a health disorder induced by a physician's treatment. Business organizations can suffer from their own "managenic" woes, caused by their leader's words, actions, or inactions. Poor supervision is one of the most important factors in employee burnout, work-performance problems, and even employee health. Researchers have discovered that mental stress is increasingly a reason for job absenteeism, and job stress is largely attributable to management-employee relations. Physicians take the Hippocratic oath, a code of behaviors that includes the caveat to "do no harm," before they begin their medical practice. Leaders' actions should follow the same ethical ideals. Loving leaders do not abdicate the accountability of leadership. They seek to do no harm, but not by ridding themselves of leadership responsibilities or blindly following someone else's theories.

Loving leaders remain in leadership roles. They share power, but do not delegate their own responsibilities away. They understand that there is a place between paternalistic authoritarianism and true empowerment that involves education and training in the accountability that comes with authority.

In a group, someone has to make the final decisions.

– Bill Walton, NBA analyst

An army of sheep led by a lion would defeat an army of lions led by a sheep.

– An Arabian proverb

[The problem with work groups is] because it's not clear who is accountable for making which decisions, it is either the brightest, most persuasive, or the biggest, meanest dude who prevails. What you end up with is the camel that was a horse designed by a committee."

– Gerald A. Kraines, Levinson Institute

Consensus is the death of leadership.

– Margaret Thatcher

You can't decentralize leadership.

– Kenneth Kaufman of Kaufman, Hall and Associates

Some managers balk at the time and expense of educating employees. With the work force destined to become transitory, they reason, why spend their company's resources on training people who will be moving on? This shortsighted viewpoint is part of what could be called the "hypocritic oath," whose adherents are bosses masquerading as leaders.

Loving the employee team includes educating them, because: (1) with training, current employees may be able to stay with the company rather than being replaced by new employees; (2) training is essential to true empowerment— empowerment to do the job to the best of one's ability and to understand the company's mission and goals in order to make decisions; and finally, (3) to educate is maternalistic.

Yes, the company may provide education to workers who use that education to move on to another job. So what? New people coming into the company will bring abilities that they may have learned through training at some other company. Maternalistic leadership is like parenting. A mother gives education to her children, who will leave her and take what she has given them, to share it with the world. As a maternalistic leader, a manager provides educational opportunities to associates who will not only be better associates while they work for their present company, but will take those skills with them wherever they go. This is loving to the individual employee

The Loving Leader:
Thoughts and Quotes

There is simply no substitute for the rewards
of helping other people grow, the pleasures
of teaching other people to succeed, and the
excitement of organizing a group of colleagues.

– Alan Loy McGinnis,
BRINGING OUT THE BEST IN PEOPLE, 1985

Leaders don't inflict pain, they bear pain.
Leadership is much more an art, a belief,
a condition of the heart, than a set of things
to do.

– Max DePree,
LEADERSHIP IS AN ART

A Chieftain's greatest reward lies in helping
Huns and Warriors prosper. Enjoying the
personal prosperity a Chieftain acquires is
only a secondary pleasure.

– VICTORY SECRETS OF ATTILA THE HUN
1993 CALENDAR (Wess Roberts, PhD)

Communication is promoted when the leader
demonstrates concern, compassion, and
sensitivity to the needs and feelings of all
group members.

– Marlys Neis and Keith Kingdon,
LEADERSHIP IN TRANSITION

> *[In hospitals that are good places to work],*
> *nurses know their administrators care and*
> *that the staff nurses' opinions are valued.*
>
> — Task Force of the American Academy
> of Nursing, Magnet Hospitals, 1983
>
> *What the workplace is ready for is leadership*
> *that truly supports people.*
>
> — Kathleen Regan and Daniel Oestreich,
> DRIVING FEAR OUT OF THE WORKPLACE

because it widens her opportunities, but it is also loving to the community because it increases the knowledge and skills of the whole. Caring management doesn't stop at the doors of the company . . . it extends into society.

Poor leadership practices affect the entire community in ways that are only beginning to be studied. For example, a variety of research studies indicate that there is a link between how people are treated at work and how they relate to their families at home. Families are directly affected by the working parent's work stress. Parents with supportive managers, clearly defined jobs, and autonomy treat their children with greater affection and esteem. They are also inclined to react to customers with more courtesy and respect.

You may believe yourself to be a loving leader. But, as your own mother probably said, actions speak louder than words. Before leaving this chapter, consider the following questionnaire and determine whether your behavior is that of a maternalistic manager.

Leadership Questionnaire #2:
Do You Love the Employee Team?

1. Do you actively think about your associates and take actions to help them stretch and grow?

2. Do you know your associates' career goals? Do you look for opportunities to help them meet these goals?

3. Are you a cheerleader for associates whether they are winning or losing?

4. Do you champion your associates' causes with other departments or higher management?

5. Do you really listen to your associates with your mind and heart?

6. Do you counsel associates on appropriate behavior, confront inappropriate behavior, give honest feedback, and discipline when necessary?

7. Do you treat all associates equitably, without prejudice or discrimination?

8. Do you share information, good and bad?

9. Do you consider the organization and its people's future when making decisions?

10. Do you accept and maintain accountability for leadership?

$\mathcal{L}$oving the Customer

There never was a customer who liked being just another number.

— Price Pritchett

"Customer service"..."service excellence"..."delightful service" ..."attentive customer relations"...these are just some of the phrases being bandied about in this era of competition. All kinds of businesses have awakened to the realization that their survival depends on their customers. Companies large and small are concentrating on how to get and keep their "share" of the market by being attentive to the needs and desires of those who purchase their goods or services. Management consultants warn of the dire consequences of ignoring customer service. In classes or seminars somewhere in America every day, employees are being taught service excellence. To the analytical mind, it may seem absurd that people have to be taught how to be polite, or that they don't automatically understand how their own job security can be affected by how they treat their customers.

Since all of us are customers, it would seem like common sense that we'd all know how to treat our own customers (i.e., simply give them the service that we would want ourselves). Besides, the consumer movement of the past few decades, coupled with all these customer-service classes, has surely transformed this country's business activities into pleasurable experiences for the patrons. Isn't that so? Well . . . most of us can at least point to some sterling examples of great service. A few companies have a reputation for consistently delivering outstanding service (Disney and Nordstrom may be the most celebrated). But superior performance in customer service is not universal. In fact, many organizations are known not for excellence, but for mediocrity.

Why isn't excellent customer service the norm? What gets in the way and prevents service excellence from being automatic? In the average company, there are five major impediments to super service:

1. A High SIQ (Self-Importance Quotient) that prevents some companies from giving customer service any importance

2. A low level of love for company employees

3. High dependence on customer-service rules

4. A low level of love and esteem for customers

5. Incompetence

The first of these impediments seems improbable today, but it is true that some companies (or at least their leaders) haven't bought in to service. They believe that their product is so essential or their competition so minimal that they needn't care about pleasing customers. They don't teach or preach customer service, nor do they value or reward their associates for providing it. Their SIQ is so high that they've forgotten why they exist.

Sometimes these companies are true monopolies and can get away with their anti-customer behavior. The demand for their services is greater than the supply; they are making profits without emphasizing service. So what if they lose a customer here or there? There are plenty more, and the bottom line is fine anyway. Henry Ford has been widely quoted as saying that his customers could have any color car they wanted . . . as long as it was black. He got rich in spite of not pandering to the public's desires. But could the company he founded succeed with such an attitude today? The question is, why would they even want to? Why would a leader want to be associated with an organization known for not caring what customers want, or with a company known for mediocre service—or mediocrity in any form? A loving leader would not.

Then again, a loving leader wouldn't have the second customer-service impediment either: a low level of love for the employees. *Wait a minute,* you might say, *that was the last chapter. We're not talking about associates here, we're talking customers.* Yes, we are, and the relationship between employee satisfaction and customer service is so direct that the one truly cannot occur without the other. There's a saying: "You can't give from an empty basket," and it applies directly to those who serve others. They cannot continue to care long-term for the needs of their customers if their own needs are being neglected. A study of Sears, Roebuck and Co. workers, reported in 1997 by the consulting company CFI Group, found that a 5 percent increase in measured employee job satisfaction translates into a 2 percent measurable improvement in customer satisfaction. Truly caring for customers requires caring for employees as well.

As a hospital executive, the author has received numerous letters about service from patients and their families. The majority have praised the nursing staff in general, as well as individual nurses for their attentiveness. They don't talk about being grateful for technology or technical skill . . . their gratitude is based on their perception that they were cared for. A few times a letter has said (more or less), "I know that the excellent care I received is a reflection of good management at your institution." One good guess is that the writers of those sentiments are managers themselves and know that the hidden work of the organization's leaders is seldom praised. Their comments have been appreciated, and we in the hospital's administration can only agree: good customer relations reflects good management-employee relations.

In the movement to provide good customer service, some managers have used rigid, autocratic rules to control

> Whenever I enter an establishment where the front-line workers seem happy, cheerful to serve, and eager to satisfy my wants, I think, "Wow, this place must have great caring leadership." Conversely, I've gone places where those earning a living from my patronage wore universally sour expressions and gave commensurate service. You know what I'm thinking about their bosses!
>
> – A service industry manager

employee behavior. When good service is provided under threat of some sort of management reprisal, it is short-lived or only occurs when the boss is present to observe it! When customer-service rules are set up, perceptions of service will improve, but service will still not be entirely satisfactory to the patron. Why? Because rules are made for general situations, not for people. True customer service isn't applied to the masses, it's of value only to the individual.

Examples of well-meaning customer service rules abound:

1. "If the diner complains about the food, remove the price of the meal from the tab."

2. "Always answer the phone: 'X company, Mary speaking, how may I help you?' "

3. "We'll cheerfully exchange anything you buy from us—no questions asked."

4. "Check the patient restrooms and be sure they're clean every fifteen minutes."

5. "Never call a patient by his first name."

Such rules do help companies make favorable impressions, but they can limit good service if they are the extent of the company's customer-relations plan. They fall short of encouraging what people usually want most of all: individual attention. Customers want their individual problem and circumstances understood, acknowledged, and paid attention to. Attentiveness is a sign of caring, and another word for caring is love. Loving leaders empower employees and encourage them to give caring attention by listening carefully to the concerns of the individual customer. They then expect employees to creatively address those concerns.

Customer-service rules or slogans are not a cure-all for organizations that want to attract business when they are not based on true concern for the customer. Just as management theory doesn't work if it's espoused as a way to manipulate associates, customer-service programs never truly succeed if they are put in place only as marketing gimmicks to manipulate customers. When are they gimmicks? When they are not founded on principles of true concern for the welfare of the people buying or using the product or service.

Customer Service on the Front Lines in America: A Reality Check

Has this ever happened to you?

You've gone to the store, post office, ticket outlet, vehicle registration office, or any other service organization and had to wait in long lines because there weren't enough checkers or clerks to serve the number of customers. After you waited in line, the clerk put up a "Closed" sign and went to lunch without serving you.

You've waited for a doctor, dentist, lawyer, or other person with whom you had an appointment and received no explanation for the delay.

You've walked into an office where the receptionist clearly sees you as an annoyance to be dealt with rather than a welcome guest.

An airline has lost your luggage.

You've called a place of business and have been immediately put on hold.

You've hunted all over the store looking for sales help, and when you locate a salesman, he's talking to another clerk about a personal matter and ignores you as you wait nearby.

You've been admitted to a hospital, dressed in a revealing gown, and told that you can't see your family when it's not visiting hours.

You've not received a reply to a letter of inquiry sent to a company.

You've had to fill out reams of paper to collect on an insurance policy or warranty you paid for.

You've paid for an insurance policy for years, and never made a claim on it, when out of the blue you get a letter in the mail saying that your policy is being cancelled: the company will no longer cover subscribers who live in your part of the country.

A mistake was made that inconvenienced you (lost luggage, late newspaper delivery, double billing), and no one ever apologized.

Loving the customer means wanting to provide a needed product, believing that the product or service is of benefit to people, and making or delivering it in a delightful manner. Companies with truly great customer service really want to serve, not simply for profit but because they care about people.

Is the idea that a company can care about its patrons idealistic? Yes. But this is the universal refrain, what we all want from those who provide our products and services: "Care about me. Care enough to provide a quality product in a quality manner." For those hard-boiled bottom-line types who scoff at this idea, guess what? The companies that care will attract the customers; it is those companies that will gather in the profits.

A marketing professional once told the author that he was the most important person in his company, because he was the one who got the product sold. Actually, I decided he was a "seller," not a "marketer," because marketing isn't selling. "Selling" implies that you convince someone that they need something, even if they don't, and get them to buy it. Most of us find that distasteful: where's the caring for me as a customer in that approach? Marketing is bigger than this. Marketing means finding out what customers want or what they say they're not getting, and then figuring out how to give it to them. There's caring in that approach.

Caring means listening to what people say they need. It means giving good service because you want to. It means individualizing that service by trying to figure out what to do for each customer's specific complaint, problem, or circumstances. It means being an ethical provider.

Ethical companies with ethical leaders provide products and services that they believe are good, safe, and needed or desired. Good, safe, and needed products? What does that mean? It means that making the quick buck is not put ahead of doing the right thing. It means that company leaders consider the lives and welfare of their customers to be just as important as their own. It means following a credo that says, "We will not knowingly do harm to others."

What a radical thought! In a country where we say things like, "Let the buyer beware," "There's a sucker born every minute," or "All's fair in love, war, and business," how can any self-respecting business person not put profit first? The question should be reversed: how can any organization's leader maintain her self-respect when she knows the company is providing a product that is not good, safe, and needed?

"Big Business" is neither respected nor trusted by the public. Too many publicized scandals and too many bad examples in the media make companies look like greedy, unprincipled monsters, willing to harm any number of people for the sake of making money. Our movies and fiction reinforce these ideas. We have come to believe that drug companies have put medications on the market when their own research revealed alarming, potentially lethal side effects; that some products were known to be harmful long before their manufacturers removed them from the market; that cigarette makers knew for decades before the rest of us that their products cause cancer. We believe that business equates to greed, and that in greed there is no place for caring about *us,* the poor, unsuspecting customers.

This perception of business has added to the cynicism and unhappiness of modern life. It has led to numerous laws and regulatory agencies that are supposed to be protecting us from the corporations. Government has to regulate and keep an eye on those who can't be trusted to do the right thing. So much of the red tape that business organizations complain about today was put in place because they or their counterparts didn't act ethically on their own.

Providing safe, high-quality products isn't the only mark

of an ethical organization. Maternal, caring organizations also take responsibility for their own actions and mistakes . . . and put customer welfare before profits. (It is certainly not a maternal instinct to poison our children or destroy their environment for a buck.)

There have been some infamous corporate-responsibility cases in the past few years, such as the Jack-in-the-Box E-coli poisonings, the Tylenol capsule poisonings, and the Exxon oil spill in Alaska. How company leaders responded to these tragedies spoke volumes about their valuation of people. While some got busy denying responsibility, others stepped up to face the problems head-on. Even when it wasn't the company's fault per se (e.g., some of the product-tampering cases), their reactions displayed either concern or greed. Concerned companies did things like pull products out of stores, which resulted in huge revenue reductions. They admitted responsibility when the error was theirs, and they apologized.

The value of a true, heartfelt apology can never be underestimated. Americans want honesty; they admire those who own up to mistakes and they are amazingly forgiving. They are much less understanding of cover-ups. Unfortunately, our legal system sometimes encourages less-than-honest treatment of others. Attorneys are horrified when their clients confess and apologize. Such behavior destroys the elaborate defense strategies with which they plan to avoid or at least minimize the money that might have to be paid out to injured parties. The author contends that there would be fewer lawsuits and less cost if companies demonstrated concern and tried to compensate victims fairly because it is the ethical thing to do, not because they're forced by a judge or jury.

H. Wayne Huizenga, Chairman of Blockbuster Entertainment, is listed in the Broward County phone book. "I'm listed because, when you are in business, people who are angry should have the right to look you up and tell you so."

– A quote from THE MIAMI HERALD

When the Weaver Popcorn Company made a mistake on 265 shipments, CEO Mike Weaver wrote every customer explaining why they goofed, how they did it, and what they were going to do in the future to repair it. Customers were flabergasted at the honesty but no one withdrew business.

– Bob Brasso and Judi Klosek,
THIS JOB SHOULD BE FUN

Should Corporations Have a Conscience?

– Headline in THE BOSTON GLOBE, April 1996

(Should we even have to ask?)

As was stated in Chapter Four, some businesses hire professional ethicists. They go to all the trouble of setting up ethics departments when what they really need is ethical, caring leaders. Some excuse their uncaring behavior as the norm, just a standard part of business, reflective of an unethical, uncaring society. They rationalize their own actions by saying "Everybody's doing it, or at least the competition is." If this is true, and one reflects the other, the question is which came first: an unethical, uncaring population, or unethical, uncaring institutions?

Big Biz Buzz: Where Is the Love?

Tobacco Industry Spends Millions Disputing Scientific Data ... R.J. Reynolds says smoking is no worse than caffeine or fatty hamburgers ...

– The Cincinnati Enquirer
(Health Science, 7/3/94)

A worker alleging he was fired after refusing to put false freshness labels on cases of chicken has sued the poultry company ... the employee alleged he was ordered to relabel the dates chickens were killed ...

– The Wall Street Journal, 2/22/95

The Federal Aviation Administration grounded about 6,000 small planes that may have "bogus" engine parts which could break and cause a crash.

– The Wall Street Journal, 3/20/95

A national survey completed in 1994 by the Healthcare Forum, the National Civic League, and DYG, Inc., found that Americans have low confidence in "virtually all leadership groups." Our society doesn't trust business leaders to have integrity. Customers listen to so many marginally truthful advertisements that they expect fraudulence. *But they don't want it.* They want honesty, respect, and concern.

Of course honesty, respect, and concern cannot take the place of competence. No matter how polite and kind the nurse is when giving an injection, the patient wants her to know what she is doing. The airline pilots on a commercial flight may be very service-oriented, but passengers also want them to be alert, oriented, drug-and-alcohol-free, and qualified to fly the plane! We want the cooks, plumbers, surgeons, teachers, dentists, waitresses, mechanics, salespeople, musicians, electricians, policemen, secretaries, fire fighters, cab drivers, social workers, telephone operators, and managers whom we deal with to be capable of doing their jobs.

Strange But True: Incompetence in the Workplace

Last year my son had a substitute teacher who couldn't read. He stumbled over words and had to have the kids in the class who were good readers take over. All the children were talking about it. I mean, that's pretty pitiful when fourth-graders have better reading skills than the teacher.

All I wanted was a second telephone line. When I called the phone company I got passed from person to person. One said her computer wasn't working so she couldn't help me. Each person I talked to was very polite, but after twenty minutes on the phone I'd talked to four people and been given three very different quotes on what the cost of the new service would be. Whatever happened to people who know how to do their jobs?

I don't go to that electronics store anymore. They're nice, but the salesmen never know anything about their products. I go where they can tell me about what they sell — the pros and cons of different brands.

My mother loved that doctor. He had the best bedside manner you could imagine — so caring, so concerned. But I HAD to sue him when his bungling killed her. I won the suit, because we proved he performed surgery he wasn't qualified to do.

Part of caring for the customer is ensuring that they will be served by people who are qualified, educated, and capable. Loving managers make it a priority to maintain a competent work team. They provide appropriate education and enforce high standards.

Maternalistic leaders have a conscience; they couldn't sleep at night if they knew they were responsible for a product or service that was harmful or fraudulent. They don't want to manipulate their customers by feigning concern in the guise of customer service; they want to provide customer service out of true concern. And that concern or love is balanced, because they have it for their companies, their associates, their customers, their communities, and themselves.

Managed care plans see all patients as essentially alike. They are units of production in a medical insurance factory...when serious illness strikes, though, we want to be treated like someone special.
— George Anders

Empathize with the customer. Try to put yourself in that person's place for just a moment.
— from a Green Spring Health Services brochure

Leadership Questionnaire #3:
Do You Love the Customers?

1. Do you provide only products or services that you are proud of, that you believe in, and that are known not to be harmful to your customers or others?

2. Do you love your employee team? (See Chapter Four.)

3. Do you pay attention to the needs and complaints of the individual customer, and encourage your associates to use creativity in solving them?

4. Do you apologize when you've made an error that affects a customer? Do you own up to mistakes, and then work to correct them?

5. Do you work to ensure that your employee team is competent as well as polite?

CHAPTER SIX

*L*oving the Community

*In and through the community lies the
salvation of the world.*

– Robert Reusing,
THE DIFFERENT DRUM

In America's political, social, and business worlds, there is a
new emphasis on *community*. We prize the maintenance of a
connected society, because its threatened loss is one more
symptom of a world less attached. In a time when many
people don't know their neighbors and spend more time
e-mailing than devoting face-to-face time with friends, we
treasure the connections brought about by a sense of our
community.

Organizations, themselves microcommunities with distinct values and cultures, are integral components of the
surrounding society. They exist as subsystems of their larger
environment. Their products or services are exchanged with
the products and services of other subsystems. They are
physically located within communities. Their customers,
employees, and bosses come from those communities. Even
if a company didn't want to interact with its environment,
it would be unable to avoid it. Each company depends (for
money, services, products, customers, employees, etc.) on

its exchanges with the community, just as the community depends on the company for jobs, products, or services.

Because a business and its community are interdependent, most companies have a basic understanding of the need for good community relations. They see favorable reputations and relationships as simply being good business. A management team is expected to possess a certain level of *savoir-faire* when dealing with the "outsiders" who make up the community external to the organization. Managers may even be evaluated on their abilities in this area.

While agreeing that good community relations is good for business, maternalistic leaders also understand that concern for the community goes beyond impressing customers to increase revenues. They understand that: (1) part of loving their associates and customers is caring about the community where they live, (2) the principles of maternalism, based on treating all people in a way that encourages their growth, cannot be limited by the walls of the organization, and (3) healthy organizations thrive in healthy communities.

The Managerial and Professional Job Functions Inventory, developed at the University of Chicago and published by London House, is a widely used tool for evaluating perceived management skills. One of the sixteen supervisory abilities it measures is "promoting community-organization relations." The MP-JFI is one example of the recognition of the importance of community relations for managers.

Loving associates and customers involves caring about the community where they live. The people who come into the organization, either to work or to receive services, live outside the company. Caring for them only while they are within the physical confines of the business would be like a parent whose only concern for her children is when they are at home. (Imagine hearing a mother say, "What they experience at school, in town, or anywhere outside of the house is of no concern to me.") Of course, managers are not responsible for personal lives, and have no input in the choices their associates make about how to live. But they can and should be concerned about the society that they and their associates live in. The conditions in the community determine the limits on lifestyle choices that can be made. The community's crime rate, social services, political scene, quality of education, and physical environment all influence the well-being of people at all levels of the organizational chart. Managers live in the community along with their associates and customers. They have personal as well as maternal reasons for caring about what goes on there.

The principles of maternalism cannot be limited by the walls of the organization. Maternalism is defined as "a way of treating people in a manner that encourages their growth and development to become their very best, most successful, most independent selves." Recalling (from Chapter One) that it's not only hands that come to work, and that the company is a subsystem with permeable walls, it is clear that concern for the surrounding environment must be a given. Employees at work cannot concentrate on doing their best when they

> *Today's breakthroughs [in management thinking] come in the form of reaching out to the community and understanding the personal and family issues that employees bring with them when they come to work every morning.*
>
> – Sam Tyler, executive producer,
> "The Excellence Files," WNET

must be concerned about the quality of child care available for their children. They may not be able to work if they are victims of crime. Their ability to thrive, both at work and in their personal lives, is directly connected to their support systems and the quality of community life.

Healthy organizations thrive in healthy communities. Health for a human being has been defined as a state of being in which he or she can function well physically, mentally, socially, and spiritually in order to express the full range of unique potentialities within the living environment. Health for a community is similar. It is a state of society where the individuals who comprise its whole can fulfill their potential. It requires opportunity, nondiscrimination, and freedom from fear of crime. An organization, as a part of the community, cannot be at its healthiest if the community as a whole is not at its healthiest, and the actions of the organization affect the health of the community as well. This interconnection creates an inherent duty for the organization to do its part to care for the community.

> *Companies do not act in isolation, as if their*
> *actions don't matter to the rest of society. Their*
> *actions matter to employees, to communities,*
> *to the earth.*
>
> – Sandra Waddock, Boston College,
> Carroll School of Management

Business leaders may take umbrage when it is suggested that they have an obligation to the community. After all, is there not already *quid pro quo*? The company gets employees and customers while the community gets jobs, products, and tax revenues. Do business entities owe something more?

Yes, if only in the sense that we all, either as individuals or as organized groups, owe a concern for the well-being of others, the consideration for future generations known as intergenerational equity, and the desire to leave our world better off than it was before we interacted with it. At the very least, companies, like individuals, have an obligation to consider how their actions influence our society, and to do what they can to avoid inflicting damage. Maternalistic industry should endeavor to care for the environment by not wasting resources, and should demonstrate a concern for the world that is to be inherited by future generations.

Concerned business leaders want to take actions that improve lives in their communities. One company that has organized a program to do just that is the Marriott Corporation. Taking to heart an obligation to improve society, Marriott recruits welfare recipients for its "Pathways to Independence" program. The formerly unemployed are given training, help with self-confidence, and—most importantly

—jobs. The program graduates more than 80 percent of those who enroll. As company chairman J. W. Marriott explains it: "We're getting good employees for the long run, but we're also helping communities."

Marriott and other like-minded companies are not simply taking over entitlement programs from the government. Rather than practicing corporate welfare, they are subscribing to the maternalistic tenet of "giving a hand, not a handout." Their contributions to the growth and development of individuals enrich the whole community.

Business and its leaders have long been stereotyped as selfish, shortsighted, and engrossed in the bottom line. We have admired businesses for their talent to make money, at the same time that we have reviled them for their apparent disregard for the community. But change is in the wind. As Henry Grunwald, the former editor-in-chief of *Time* magazine, has said, "Talent without humanity is not worth having." Companies and their leaders are beginning to demonstrate their humanity through what they give, not only to their own company families but to the larger community family.

Marriott has chosen its Pathways education as a specific program for service. Other management teams can care for

> *This we know: the earth does not belong to man, man belongs to the earth. All things are connected like the blood that unites us all. Man did not weave the web of life, he is merely a strand in it. Whatever he does to the web, he does to himself.*
>
> – Chief Seattle

their communities by utilizing their own talents in their own chosen ways. The following are some actions that would indicate a company's community-service inclination (of course, this is only a partial list of ideas):

1. The encouragement of managers and associates to volunteer for community programs and nonprofit organizations

2. Company recognition of employees who volunteer for community programs

3. The encouragement and recognition of employees who are active in service clubs

4. Financial and in-kind (such as loaned executives) donations to community organizations like the United Way

5. Business mentoring programs for community youth

6. Involvement in business-elected official coalitions working to solve community problems

7. Policies providing for time away from work for volunteer projects. (One company that says it reaps rewards from just such a policy is Timberland, the boot and clothing maker, which pays employees for five days of community service every year. Executives say that in helping the community they are also gaining skills for their employees through the volunteer projects.)

8. The provision of educational scholarships to community members

9. Hiring practices that honor the abilities and potential of all community members

Maternalistic leaders work to improve society. They try to prevent the breakdown of communities. They understand the value of prevention—that the cost of preventative actions is minuscule compared to the costs of curing a community that is already sick.

Why, then, should business leaders give to their communities? Perhaps they can borrow an idea from community park board member Jesse Turner, of Bremerton, Washington, who when asked by a reporter why she gives her heart and soul to the community, responded: "Service is the rent we pay for living." In the same way, service is the rent that companies pay for being a part of the community.

> *In our nation's capital, community is a buzzword. Across the country, people talk of rebuilding and sustaining a connection between people, a sense of belonging to place and each other.*
>
> – Ellen Goodman, THE BOSTON GLOBE, 8/7/97
>
> *We spend a lot of time, money, and energy responding to the symptoms of broken communities.*
>
> – Oregon congressman Earl Blumehauer

Leadership Questionnaire #4:
Do You Love the Community?

1. Do you and your company consciously avoid polluting the environment or wasting natural resources?

2. Do you volunteer time, money, or talent to community service groups ?

3. Do you encourage and recognize employees who volunteer their time, money, or talent to community-service groups?

4. Do you participate with other leaders in planning for the community's future?

$\mathcal{L}$oving the Leader

If an individual is able to love productively,
he loves himself, too; if he can love only
others, he cannot love at all.
— Eric Fromm

Self-love is often confused with selfishness and
conceit. We are selfish when we do not love
and accept ourselves, and attempt to take from
others to fill the gap. Take good care of yourself
now so you can care about the rest of us.

— Jennifer James

Management books and parenting books share many concepts, one of which is an emphasis on the welfare of others. For parents the accent is on caring for their children's needs; for leaders it is on contributing to the growth and development of subordinates. Most of these books forget to discuss what Fromm and James refer to above: the importance of self-love.

One might think that managers must feel good about themselves, in order to have climbed the corporate ladder. After all, it takes self-esteem to believe you have what it takes to lead. This line of reasoning is faulty because of the way many people end up in leadership roles. Some fall into management; they are the best technicians or workers in their departments, so supervisors assume that they should move up. Some had to be talked into taking the job. Others see management as the only route open for advancement in the company (or more money), or see it as a way to escape from work they don't enjoy. For every manager who planned her career as a boss, there is another who simply found herself there, at least at the lower levels of supervision.

Even those whose career goals originally included leadership may not have the self-confidence that they project. An interesting phenomenon is the impostor syndrome shared by many successful people from all walks of life. Impostor-syndrome leaders secretly believe that they don't deserve their status. They perceive themselves to be frauds who could be found out by others at any time.

Whether her management career was planned or serendipitous, a boss has special needs for self-esteem, for two distinct reasons. The first has been documented by social scientists for years: those who cannot care for themselves cannot care for others. The second is described in Chapter One: bosses, just because they are bosses, are subject to the antipathy of others. Without self-love, they cannot possibly continue to practice loving leadership day after day.

Dealing With Reality: To Love Doesn't Always Mean to BE Loved

A supervisor once approached her manager with a dejected demeanor and said she was considering leaving her job. She was sad and disillusioned because of recent events with the employees in her department. It was union contract bargaining time. Some of the things being said by the union and by her own associates were hurtful and, to her mind, blatantly untrue.

"I don't understand it," she said. "I think I'm an enlightened leader. I share information and power with people . . . I care about them and go to bat for them with upper management. I work so hard to make things better for them . . ." She was disappointed and angry because she felt unloved and unappreciated by those from whom she expected gratitude.

The manager knew this supervisor very well, and considered her perceptions of her own leadership style to be accurate. She *was* a loving leader; she cared deeply about the company, the customers, and the employees. She practiced the art and science of management with great skill. The problem was that she made an assumption that many of us make: that her loving attitude would be universally returned.

Well, it doesn't work that way, as those who choose to practice loving leadership find out. Those who expect universal appreciation face certain disappointment. Caring for others is no assurance that they will care for you.

People with strong needs for positive affirmation from others don't do well as loving leaders. They're not going to have their adulation needs met, because:

✦ Management is not a popularity contest. Loving decisions that must be made for the good of the customers, the company, and the employees will not please everyone.

✦ Maternalistic leaders encourage growth in others. Growth comes with pain, hard work, mistakes, and change. Change can lead to anger and resentment. When offering growth opportunities to others, the maternalistic manager may hear: "Why are you making me do this? It's not *my* job. You're the one getting paid the big bucks!" Similarly, do teenagers appreciate parents for enforcing rules or delegating duties in an attempt to help their offspring grow into responsible adults? Some do, some do but won't say so, and some definitely don't!

✦ The more you do for others, the more they expect you to do for them. Just as children can become spoiled by all that their parents do for them, associates become spoiled by fair, caring leaders. The American child who becomes angry or feels mistreated because his dinner is chicken and not a hamburger, forgets to be grateful that he even has a dinner. It doesn't occur to him to appreciate the fact that he was born in a country and a family that can afford to feed him. Adults have the same shortsightedness. How many of us remember to count our blessings regularly? How many in this country remember how lucky they are to be Americans? People who have the good fortune to work with caring leaders often develop a sense of entitlement that causes them to expect and demand more from those leaders.

✦ Many people have so many needs themselves—for esteem, praise, love—that they are unable to give these things to others. (We say that such people are unable to give from an empty basket.) Whether it is due to self-absorption, jealousy of those more successful, anti-establishment rebelliousness, the pervasive American belief in entitlement, or simple human nature, it seems that it is easy for us to recognize bad or unfair treatment, while good leadership is invisible. We may not even notice it. And the best, most maternalistic, loving leaders make it look so easy that we don't realize how hard it can be to be "The Boss."

When confronted with these attitudes, leaders who expect and need gratitude may become disillusioned or angry. More than one who started out with every intention of being a transformational, mentoring boss has become cynical over time. Then he has either left management or, more often, becomes an unloving, laissez-faire, stereotypical bad boss.

Loving, maternalistic leadership is hard work. It calls for unconditional love, which means continuing to understand with no guarantee of being understood. It cannot be practiced by those who need to be universally liked or those with strong codependency needs. (Codependent people must be assured that they are needed, and they work to keep things that way.) It requires consistent role modeling of integrity, competence, and superior interpersonal skills. It takes ability, knowledge, ethics, humor, and courage.

Courage is required because change management and confrontation, however skillfully applied, lead to criticism. To talk about actually loving an organization and its people goes against the grain of the business world. In fact, loving leaders run the risk of being seen as not worthy of leadership because they are "too soft" and not sufficiently concerned about the stockholders' profits. They may not seem "believable" to burned-out, suspicious workers whose corporate acculturation has convinced them that whatever tack the boss takes is yet another form of subordinate manipulation.

Other managers, their peers, may see them as easy targets for turf takeovers. Maternalistic leaders are often viewed opportunistically. They may be seen as competitors who can be readily outdone for the best assignments or promotions. They're so concerned with doing the right thing for the company, clients, and staff that they can be surpassed and undermined by those whose sole goal is self-promotion. The use of political maneuvering rather than quality work and unethical behavior rather than a straightforward addressal of problems is so unthinkable to the loving leader that others see these ploys as powerful weapons to be used against her. Unloving leaders can view maternal managers as naive, stupid "saps" who can be easily sabotaged in the competition for promotion and company recognition.

Although the maternalistic leader might be seen as weak by her bosses, a manipulative fraud by her subordinates, and a pushover by her peers, these are faulty perceptions, because:

1. It is the exceptionally strong, not the weak, who can take the difficult road of maternalism. Weaker leaders take the easier, well-worn path of bosses before them by falling into step with "the big boys," by taking on the jokes, cultures, prejudices, competitive motives, and traditional management styles of the establishment.

2. Loving leaders practice leadership theory because they care, not from any need to manipulate.

3. Part of loving is to love yourself . . . which means possessing self-esteem. People with high self-esteem aren't naive dupes; they are what we call "their own persons," with extensive knowledge of themselves.

Self-esteem, as much as it is talked about these days, is still largely underrated in its importance. If we were to diagram any human action or interaction the way we learned to diagram sentences, virtually 100 percent of them would have to include self-esteem or its lack, just as a sentence must contain a verb. Self-esteem might be one of the principle features of a human event or only a contributing factor, but it would have to be included somewhere in the diagram. In analyzing interpersonal relationships, it cannot be overlooked. It also can't be overstated: *self-esteem is just as important as communication skills in determining the success of interpersonal relationships.*

A. Protagonists: Boss and Subordinate

ACTION: The boss will not share information and will not "brag" about subordinates' superior performance to others.

RATIONALE FOR ACTION: "If I share information with this superior employee or let others know how good he is, he might be promoted above me."

UNDERLYING MOTIVATION: Low self-esteem of Boss. "I'm not good enough to maintain my job if someone else is seen as outstanding."

B. Protagonists: Department Head A & Department Head B

ACTION: "Turf" battles as the company restructures. Each claims that quality will suffer if the other manager gains control of an area currently included in the colleague's department. Neither will consider what is best for the entire company.

RATIONALE FOR ACTION: Maintenance of self-esteem requires each to cling to turf. "If my area becomes smaller, I will be less important."

C. Protagonists: Abuser and Victim (may be verbal abuse, spousal abuse, or harassment)

ACTION: Victim allows abuse to continue.

RATIONALE FOR ACTION: "I deserve no better" or "I'm not strong enough to do anything about it."

D. Protagonists: A Female Loving Leader and Her Female Protege

ACTION: Protege admires her mentor but feels that her mentor should not be promoted to CEO.

RATIONALE FOR ACTION: Protege's own lack of self-esteem as a female leads her to believe that a CEO must be male, no matter how competent her mentor is. The lack of belief in her own ability can be sublimated to complaint when a male is promoted: "You see, it doesn't matter how good we are. See how good J is, and they still won't promote a woman. I don't have a chance."

Whenever self-esteem and managers are considered together, two misconceptions are common. The first, mentioned previously, is the unwarranted belief that leaders automatically have self-esteem. The second confuses self-love with egocentricity.

The low self-esteem of some people in business-leadership positions causes problems for their company and colleagues. Managers who don't feel good about themselves are threatened by any embarrassment. They cannot apologize. They cannot help others climb the corporate ladder, for fear that mentees will do better in life than their mentors. One type of Low Self-Esteem Boss (LSEB) is unable to admit making a mistake. That inability interferes with the organization's success, because she will not consider changing her mind once a course of action has been determined—even when new information indicates a need for change. Other LSEBs are unable to make decisions, for fear of making a mistake.

High self-esteem is a prerequisite for success as a loving leader. In fact, every individual's potential for success is a direct derivative of his own self-esteem. Self-esteem is essential in order to survive inevitable conflict and criticism. Having it does not mean wearing a superiority complex. In fact, the SIB (Self-Important Boss) with a high SIQ (Self-Importance Quotient) is a product of low self-esteem. Self-worth allows individuals to value others, not feel superior to them. People with a sense of worthiness are the only ones not vulnerable to every slight, criticism, or self-perceived imperfection. They know themselves, and have evaluated both their strengths and weaknesses. They can practice humility while those with low self-esteem are busy protecting themselves behind a variety of facades, sometimes including a sort of self-chauvinism. Humility, or being humble, is not the same thing as being a martyr. Leaders with high self-esteem are able to care for others while caring for and respecting themselves.

> Who is expected to leap tall corporate problems in a single bound and solve office squabbling faster than a speeding bullet? Why, supermanager, of course. It's no wonder, then, that so many managers privately feel unequal to to the task of running their companies or departments.
>
> – Columnist Carol Smith

The Boss and Self-Esteem

The High Self-Esteem Boss	The Low Self-Esteem Boss
Accepts feedback, criticism, and bad news as important information for her or the company's growth.	Will not allow criticism or bad news to be delivered. Sees these as personal attacks and becomes defensive.
Rewards those who bring information, whether it is good or bad.	Rewards only those who bring good news, flattery, and praise for boss and company.
Empowers, is able to share information, and allows others to take risks.	Micromanages everything and everyone.
Encourages the growth and education of others.	Does not assist others in their growth and education.
Is able to apologize.	Has never been heard to say, "I made a mistake."
Can change her mind when given data, evidence.	Has never been heard to publicly change her mind, either because she will not permit data and evidence to be given to her, or because she disregards it.
Truly believes in (and demonstrates) the value of every employee.	Truly believes that value is determined by position on the organizational chart.

Self-Care

Self-love is manifested by self-care, which is about "leading yourself" in the way that you want to be led. It means mothering yourself the way you want to be mothered. To mother means to watch over, nourish, and protect, with concern for growth and development, health, and happiness. Practicing maternalism on yourself ranges from living a well-balanced life to fostering your own self-growth, and it includes a concern for physical health.

Because managers tend to have trouble balancing their personal lives with their working lives, they can easily fall into workaholism. Balance is achieved when time and energy are devoted to both the work world and the home-life world. Workaholics are typically intense, driven, and energetic. They compete with others and with themselves. They put in many more hours at their job than the typical American considers to be full time. They don't "waste" time and they seem to be addicted to work. Theories about how they got to be this way abound. One is that early childhood conditioning taught them that their parents' love and approval was based on their ability to meet high standards of success. As they grew into adulthood, their self-esteem needs dictated that they be better than others or as close to perfect as possible, due to a fear of failure. Workaholics have been admired and valued by their companies because of their perceived productivity. Indeed, some are remarkably productive. But at what price is this productivity obtained?

For some leaders—those who are truly happy when they're working—workaholism may not lie outside the realm of self-care. But for many more, putting in long workdays that leave no time for a personal life is a prescription for lifelong disequilibrium. The best leaders are those who lead balanced lives themselves. They have a broader perspective of the world and a better comprehension of their associates' life-balancing needs. Social scientists of all persuasions agree that self-loving people are well-rounded people, not one-dimensional bosses who live only to work.

According to Dr. Gerald Kushel of the Institute for Effective Thinking, only 4 percent of people enjoy both their work and their family lives. Leaders who love themselves don't settle for joining that 96-percent majority; they seek fulfillment in all of life. Their self-care includes paying attention to their personal lives and devoting time to making "home" a source of strength and happiness. This requires attention to their families, which means a dedication of time. The classic workaholic doesn't allot that time to anything outside of the job. The maternalistic leader does, because he realizes that balance is essential to health and because he takes good care of himself.

Concern for good health is paramount to self-care. Healthy individuals care for themselves by remaining attentive to their emotional, spiritual, and physical needs, and by taking action to ensure that those needs are met. In effect, they *nurse* themselves (another word associated with maternalism) by regularly assessing all areas of their existence, diagnosing any problem (or unhealthy) areas, and planning and carrying out a course of treatment to maintain a healthy life.

Maternalistically healthy living includes:

+ **Balance,** an equilibrium between the job and home life. A balanced life includes hobbies,

friendships, vacations and other recreational
activities, and loving relationships.

+ **Physical maintenance**, which requires exercise,
a healthful, well-balanced diet, adequate rest and
sleep, weight maintenance, appropriate physical
examinations, and avoidance of "health robbers"
such as drugs, nicotine, excessive alcohol, and
indiscriminate sexual activity.

+ **Spiritual maintenance**, or attending to spiritual
or religious needs (including refusal to do work
that conflicts with the soul's needs and ethics).

+ **Stress management**, through understanding
what causes stress at home and at work and
learning techniques to prevent it from affecting
physical and emotional health.

+ **Self-growth and development**, through the recognition that growth and learning are essential to
life. In these less than certain times, the dedication
to self-improvement includes staying in charge of
your own employability.

The number of self-development books on the market
and the increasing number of working people returning to
school indicate a widespread acknowledgment that education
doesn't end at adulthood. Who buys these books and takes
these classes? Those who feel they've "made it" or those who
are trying to climb a corporate ladder?

In one of this author's graduate classes, classmates were
amazed when I said I was back in college to make myself

better in my current position, not to prepare for a new job. To the man (and they were mostly men), they were in school to obtain letters after their names so that they could move up or go into a new career. They didn't understand the rationale that someone in a job she loved needed to be back in school to maintain current knowledge and sharp thinking skills. They seemed to think, as do many people, that once you've been promoted into the management job you want, "you don't have to go to school anymore."

Of course, those students were right, you *don't* have to go to school anymore. But, if you are truly loving yourself you will never stop your schooling (whether it's done in a university, via continuing education classes, or through self-directed study). Self-nurturing means seeking growth, both because all organisms have a need for growth and because of the recognition that anyone who is not growing in today's slushy, changing world will not be able to maintain a current position or be prepared for the new jobs. Thriving requires practicing futurism by getting ready for the future for your own benefit, too.

Self-growth requires an analysis of personal strengths and weaknesses. The weaknesses must be acknowledged and worked on! Just as organizations have projects for Continuous Quality Improvement, so should the individual have a personal CQI plan. This includes a plan of action. It requires knowing who you are and being willing to work to improve yourself.

Maternalistic leaders don't stop at recognition of their areas of needed growth. They also understand their own strengths. They are proud of their accomplishments and they celebrate their victories. They privately pat themselves on the back for successful projects, even when others don't recognize their part in them. (And that can happen frequently to managers who may be behind the scene, making their associates' progress possible.) They know how to compliment themselves.

In fact, they appreciate themselves with self-rewards. They treat themselves the way they would want their parents to treat them. That includes giving themselves unconditional love. They don't practice perfectionism, which can lead to either an inability to recognize (and thereby correct) weaknesses or a kind of self-hate when the flaws are recognized. They give themselves tolerance and forgiveness for imperfections. They support themselves with kindness and positive "self talk." They do not stay in jobs, relationships, or situations that are unhealthy for them. They love themselves: the prerequisite for loving others.

Loving the Leader's Leader

One of those others who need love is the leader's leader, another person usually forgotten in management "how to" books. Maternalistic leaders nurture not only downward to associates (in the classical hierarchical organizational chart), sideward to peers, and inward to self, they nurture upward to their supervisor.

Loving the boss means treating him with courtesy, kindness, and honesty. It does not mean "brown-nosing," flattery, or political behavior—all forms of manipulation for self-gain. It is based on one simple rule: treat the boss the way you want those to whom you are the boss to treat you.

Managers who are very aware from their own experience that it can be lonely at the top sometimes forget that this holds true for their bosses, as well—and maybe to an even greater extent. After all, the boss's boss is at a higher "top." The very same person who remembers to compliment subordinates on a job well done may never give praise to her superior. It's too easy to either forget that the boss has the same human needs to be cared about, or believe that such care would not be welcomed. Loving the leader includes:

- ✦ **Looking out for the boss's best interests.** This includes such things as keeping her well-informed and alerted to potential problems. It includes speaking well of her to others and not complaining about her or blaming her to subordinates for unpopular decisions or company rules.

- ✦ **Communicating honestly.** It's been said of executives that the day they received their promotions into upper management was the last day they heard the truth. No one wants to take bad news to the Big Boss. No one wants to confront her when they disagree with her decisions. But not only is it unloving to the supervisor to withhold bad news or neglect to give her input about decisions, it is unloving to the organization, the customers, and the other employees. Because the leader's decisions affect everyone, it is unfair to her and to the company to give her incomplete information on which to base these decisions. To allow fear of her reactions to get in the way of honest input amounts to sabotage.

+ **Support the boss's decisions.** Voicing opinions, including disagreement, is the responsible, loving thing to do. But disagreements should be aired in an appropriate forum: the private office or a meeting where input is solicited. Once the boss has clearly articulated that she has heard the opposing views and has made a final decision, her "call" becomes the management team's "call." The loving manager's role is to understand the rationale for her boss's decision so she can explain it to others as the company's decision. Her job is not to say, "I disagree with this, but the boss says we have to do it her way."

+ **Knowing the boss's strengths and weaknesses.** The loving manager knows that no one is perfect, and that the boss will make mistakes. Maternalism means forgiving those mistakes, and contributing personal strengths to supplement the boss's abilities.

+ **Reward the boss.** Everyone needs to be appreciated, thanked, and praised. Honest, specific compliments for a job well done and honest appreciation for a boss's leadership will help the boss continue to grow and thrive.

Of course, loving the leader is easier if the leader is also of the maternalistic persuasion. The boss's boss who welcomes input, openly asks for information (good and bad), supports other people's growth, seeks self-understanding, and truly loves the company and its people will understand and welcome the caring associate.

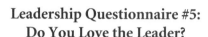

Leadership Questionnaire #5:
Do You Love the Leader?

1. Do you understand that concerned and loving behavior may not be reciprocated, but choose to behave with love anyway?

2. Do you forgive yourself when you make a mistake?

3. Do you forgive your boss when he makes a mistake?

4. Do you feel worthy of your own success?

5. Do you lead a balanced life by dividing your time and energy between work life and home life?

6. Do you care for your body with a good diet, exercise, and rest?

7. Do you appreciate yourself and reward yourself for your contributions to the organization?

8. Do you treat and support your boss the way you want to be treated and supported?

CHAPTER EIGHT

*D*eveloping More Loving Leaders

Not all of us have to possess earthshaking talent.
Just common sense and love will do.

– Myrtle Auvil

In a perfect world, maternalism would be the practice of everyone in the company, but of course the world isn't perfect. There is no perfect organization and no perfect boss. Maternalistic leaders understand this. Rather than bemoan this imperfection, they make it a lifelong quest to increase loving leadership. This chapter addresses strategies for moving toward a more widespread practice of maternalism in the workplace.

How to Measure a Company's Loving Leadership Quotient

In 1953, author Ashley Montagu made the observation that, in the human species, "survival is more closely tied to the capacity for love and cooperation than to anything other."[1]

---

[1] Montagu, Ashley. *The Natural Superiority of Women.* New York: Macmillan Co., 1953.

In 1972, Virginia Satir's opinion was that, "We are in the beginning of another evolution in the history of man. Probably never before have so many people been so discouraged and dissatisfied with the state of the human condition as now. Everywhere people are demanding change. The main cry needs to be for greater feelings of individual self-esteem and the loving, nurturing contexts that go with it."[2]

Today's workplaces, as microcosms of the larger society, are models of what both writers had to say: an organization's survival is tied to the capacity for love and cooperation, and many of today's workers are discouraged, dissatisfied, and in need of the loving, nurturing contexts of maternalism. In some places, they're getting it, even when managers don't know that they're practicing it:

Mitchell Rabkin, CEO of Beth Israel of Boston, practices maternalism by ensuring that all employees treat each other with respect and that all patients receive warm, personalized care. The result: Beth Israel has a national reputation for excellence.

Howard Schultz, CEO of Starbucks, the coffee shop chain, bases his management on treating employees well. He believes that profitability and good treatment of employees (called partners) go hand in hand. The result of his practice of building employee loyalty has been a business "phenomenon." (USA WEEKEND)

---

[2] Satir, Virginia. *Peoplemaking.* Palo Alto, California: Science and Behavior Books, 1972.

Marriott International, Inc., is committed to a
welfare-to-work program that improves the
community and changes the lives of individuals:
"Marriott nurtures workers by driving welfare
trainees to work, arranging daycare, negotiating
with landlords, dealing with caseworkers, buying
clothes, visiting them at home, and coaching them
in everything from banking skills to self-respect."
(THE WALL STREET JOURNAL, 10/31/96)

Whole Food Market, Inc., which owns New England's
Bread and Circus chain, believes in developing the
skills of all employees. As an "employee democracy,"
the company makes its decisions based on employee
votes.

Southwest Airlines has the best on-time record and
baggage service of comparable airlines. Executives
practice what they say: "A company bound by love,
or at least mutual respect, will fare much better"
than others. (The NEW YORK TIMES news service)

Loving leaders can be found in many companies (whether
or not they've clearly articulated their beliefs), but an organization does not become a totally nurturing environment
until enough of the leadership team believes and practices this
kind of management. What's needed to develop and maintain
a maternalistic workplace is a critical mass, or a large enough
number of people to collectively change the company's culture. Of course, the higher the level of individual power, the
smaller the number of people needed to achieve this.

When I talked about things that had deeper meaning, like communicating differently, treating people the right way, I found a lot of the time I was taking it on the chin from upper management.

— A former corporate VP and CFO, quoted by
Hal Lancaster, THE WALL STREET JOURNAL

If the CEO and other top managers want a maternalistic company, the changes needed to encourage the development of maternalism will likely occur quickly. This demonstrates that a company's board of directors is extremely powerful in determining the company's ethics, principles, relationship mores, and everyday working rules, even though they may believe they're far removed from them. Board members are not blameless, as many like to believe, if a company's culture is less than ethical, quality-oriented, and nurturing. The board selects the top corporate managers—the people in the organization with the greatest direct power, and therefore the highest influence factor. This is an even greater responsibility than their commonly quoted "fiscal responsibility."

Because of the stronger influence that can thus be brought into play, what is optimal for the development of loving leadership is support from the top of the organization. But maternalism can begin to change a company at any level of management. Anyone who is called a manager manages something for the company, so he or she has the power to affect the working lives of at least one group of people. A maternalistic manager can set standards and expectations within his own sphere of influence, whether that be an office, a work team, a department, or a division. He can serve as a role model for others in his sphere and adjoining spheres. Together with other leaders, he can create the critical mass that can change an organization's culture. After all, organizations are systems. According to systems theory, a change in any part of the system causes an automatic change in the entire system. If a critical mass is reached—if enough people, or parts of the system, change—the whole system will be significantly changed.

An organization is made up of people. Its culture is an amalgam of all those people's beliefs and values. The culture defines how people work in the organization. It determines how power is divided, how much risk is tolerated, how decisions are made, how company resources are allocated, and how people are managed. Each person's position in the company, or rather, his *relative* position to all of the other people at work, determines how much influence his particular values will have on the overall culture.

Formal leaders are imbued with positional power because of their place in the organization, relative to everyone else. So, of course, a leader high up on the company's organizational chart has more cultural influence than a first-line manager. If *enough* leaders with *enough* combined influence think alike, they have the potential to determine the workplace culture.

There's no magical number for determining how much leadership influence equals the power to change the culture of a particular company. The following chart illustrates how comparative ratios of "culturepower" could add up to a critical mass to influence the culture. If we arbitrarily assign the company president 100 culturepower "points," the company vice presidents 50 points, department heads 20 points, informal (nonmanager) leaders 15 points, first-line supervisors 10 points, and nonmanagement employees 2 points, then:

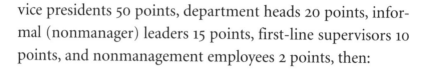

Loving Leadership Cultural Influence

1 president (100 points) would equal 2 vice presidents

or 5 department heads

or 6 informal leaders

or 10 front-line supervisors

or 50 employees

The relative value or relative influence among individuals in a workplace differs from organization to organization. The point-weight given to various levels may not be the same, but the formula works in any company. The message is this: while many claim that there must be support from the very top in order for any organizational change to occur, the cultural shift to a maternalistic organization can originate at any level of a management team, if that level has enough loving leaders. Major changes and company decisions may come from the top, but culture is influenced by every person in the organization. The challenge for those lower in the hierarchy is to have the courage to persevere and to team with others who share the same values. This perseverance takes courage because, as we have seen, companies and society do not tend to give visible rewards to those who choose maternalism. In spite of what people say they want; in spite of common sense and professional golden rules, rewards still seem to go to those focused on getting to the top, rather than to those who are doing the right thing for employees, customers, and the company. This will continue in your company, unless enough leaders change the culture.

This book should probably have been preceded by another entitled *Living With Love: Maternalism for the Modern World,* because all organizations are subsystems of the larger systems variously called community, society, nation, world, and universe. It would be so much easier to promote loving leadership in business if maternalism were as valued in our culture as prestige, power, and money. Nurturing contexts would be more natural for adults in the workplace if they were indigenous to all organizations, from families to schools to government entities. When they are not, it is an essential challenge for leaders to improve their own maternalistic skills, help develop other loving leaders, and seek the necessary critical mass that will ensure a culture where the company, customers, managers, and nonmanagement staff can all grow and thrive.

At the top of a traditional corporate organization chart is the board of directors. As was mentioned above, their part in setting a culture is much greater than it is usually considered to be. Boards select a least the top employee of the company—the CEO or president; sometimes they select other key executives as well. Some organizations (particularly nonprofits) have more involved boards than others. That is, they're more involved (at least superficially) in the actual operations of the company. But in many cases, boards hire executives and then act as business advisors, concerned primarily with financial reports and strategic planning. These are appropriate roles for boards. In addition, board members who really love the company will make it a priority to hire executives who also really love the company, its customers, and its employees. Then they will observe to see if the working CEO is really the person they thought they hired. That is, do her actions match their expectations of a loving leader?

The easiest way to improve the level of maternalism in an organization is to hire loving people. Of course, that's more easily said than done. How is the manager or team that is doing the hiring to know how a job applicant feels about the company, himself, and other people? One way is to ask. Both reference checks and job interviews should be designed to elicit information about the would-be employee's dedication, passion, ethics, and interpersonal skills. This information is just as important as details of job skills and past experience. It is essential data in determining if an individual's personal philosophy mirrors the organization's. Questions normally asked when a manager is being hired should also be asked of the entry-level employee. Those beginning workers are the pool from which future managers will be promoted. They should be hired with an eye to their long-term potential as well as their ability to do the current job. Even those whose aspirations don't include management will bring culture "points" to the company that may change the cultural balance. Their beliefs about work, others, and themselves are important to know and weigh.

The following is a list of sample reference or interview questions for potential team members.

- ✦ What do you want to be doing for this company
  in one year, five years, ten years?

✦ How can I, as your new manager, help you reach your goals?

✦ How will you, as a team member, help others reach their goals?

✦ How do you feel about this company and its mission statement?

✦ How do you feel about our product or service?

✦ Describe your ideal job.

✦ Describe the ideal workplace.

✦ Describe an interpersonal conflict you've had and how you dealt with it.

✦ What would you do if I, your new manager, asked you to do something you considered unethical? (What would you consider to be unethical?)

✦ Explain your personal philosophy of management.

A philosophy is a system of values and beliefs that influences everything about the way a person lives life. While some people think about philosophy in the large context of religion, or personal life, it is management philosophy that determines where energy and emphasis are placed at work.

This book is about a philosophy called maternalism, but that term is just a name—a descriptor of a particular set of beliefs and actions. Everyone has an individual belief system, even though they may not have named their philosophy or analyzed how their basic theories about life dictate their behavior and relationship with their world. When a group of individuals agree on their shared values, they are able to develop a common philosophy that is the basis for group decisions and interactions. Mature people have philosophies that they are able to articulate to others. Mature groups, too, are able to develop shared philosophies that they can articulate so that others can determine whether they subscribe to the same values and norms.

Part of the hiring process should be to make sure that the applicant knows what he'd be getting himself into (warts and all!) if he chose to join the company. It does no favor to the applicant or the company if he's hired with an unrealistic understanding of the company or the job. Many applicants or new hires are given the company's mission statement, but few receive the management philosophy. That's probably because so few written company management philosophies exist.

Large and small companies all over the country spend big bucks sending their designated leaders to classes so they'll become "better managers" without ever defining what "better management" is. Some of these companies try to hold their managers to standards, or include management skills as part of annual evaluations, without defining what those standards and skills should be. Their top leaders erroneously believe that merely by having a mission statement, they have provided guidance for management decision making.

In order for a culture to become widely maternalistic, there must be a shared philosophy that is understood and followed. From the company's philosophy should come standards for performance for every person in the organization.

The mission statement tells why the company exists, i.e., what its purpose is. The philosophies determine the behaviors of those whose duty it is to carry out the mission. A maternalistic company might have several philosophies, but would certainly have at least two: a customer-based philosophy and a management philosophy. From the philosophies and mission statement come the organization's goals, decision-making rules, and job standards. Each manager's annual evaluation should then include how well she meets written standards, including those that deal with leadership competence.

A Sample Customer Philosophy

We Believe That:

+ Quality products and customer service must be our priority. Company decisions will be based on this priority.

+ Customers deserve, and should receive from us, individualized attention to their needs and concerns.

+ In order to provide excellent quality and service, we must maintain a dedicated, competent work force.

A Sample Management Philosophy

We Believe That:

+ Management is a valid professional specialty, and that managers have the responsibility to become educated and to maintain current knowledge about management and leadership.

+ Every associate in this organization is a valuable employee deserving of respect.

✦ Managers, as leaders, should be role models and mentors to those we supervise, striving to assist them in their personal growth and learning.

✦ We should strive to be fair and equitable in our management decisions, realizing that some decisions may not be widely popular, and that employee disciplinary action is sometimes necessary.

✦ In all communications with those we supervise, we must be cognizant of the importance of maintaining associate self-esteem. We will treat each individual with respect. Even in times of employee discipline, we will make every effort to preserve the employee's sense of self-worth.

✦ The company is enriched by diversity of skills. We will appreciate this diversity by respecting all employees and by utilizing their talents in their areas of expertise.

✦ All people fail at something sometimes, and that no person is a perfect worker, employee, or manager. Knowing this, we strive to show kindness and forgiveness to our colleagues, and to ourselves.

Sample Job Standards for a Maternalistic Manager

At a Minimum, a Manager in This Company:

✦ Is considerate and respectful in all interactions with customers and team members (meaning all other employees).

✦ Demonstrates dedication to service excellence by taking immediate and specific actions to correct organizational blocks to excellence and to improve service.

✦ Listens and seeks to understand the concerns of customers and team members. Actively seeks feedback, both positive and negative, about the company *and* his or her own performance.

+ Promotes personal and professional growth and development of team members through specific actions.

+ Accepts accountability for the success of the entire organization. Does not make decisions based on the preservation of "personal turf."

+ Serves as an advocate of the company, the customers, *and* the employees. Each manager's proposals and decisions will include documentation that the welfare of each party involved was considered in the decision-making process.

+ Encourages creativity among team members by welcoming new ideas, carefully considering all proposals, and rewarding those associates who propose and/or attempt innovations.

+ Displays added-value behavior by using good problem-solving techniques, including respectful use of confrontation skills, maintenance of confidentiality, and actions that establish and maintain an environment of honesty and trust.

A set of beliefs is useless if it is not shared, understood, and followed. It's not enough to hire people who seem to share the organization's valued norms; their behavior must then mirror their values. The importance of holding others accountable to behave in harmony with shared values has been described in Chapter Four; this accountability should be clear from the day of hire. Periodic performance evaluations of all managers should include assessments of management skills and of the adherence to standards. Much havoc has been caused by managers who haven't been monitored by *their* managers and haven't been held accountable to the company's espoused values. Formal leaders, as well as front-line workers, need growth opportunities that include counseling and discipline.

Some managers aren't hired from outside the company, but move up from within. Promoting from inside the organization is a positive indication that a company is "growing its own," but a look at *who* gets promoted is indicative of the company's real values. In an unloving organization, it may be the politically correct employee who becomes the boss, rather than the person with true leadership skills. Americans joke about this with sayings like, "It's not what you know, it's who you know." In a loving organization, promotions go to loving leaders, not those whose greatest talent lies in internal political maneuvers.

To increase the loving leadership quotient, neither should promotion into management be solely based on technical skills. Any assessment of management potential should include the individual's beliefs and actions in support of the management philosophy. An organization trying to change by reaching critical mass or an organization already practicing loving leadership must consider this with every manager choice. Promotion automatically grants cultural influence points to management because of the positional power that accompanies formal leadership roles.

Positional power is an important aspect of leadership. It isn't like personal power that derives from an individual's personality, charisma, and behavior. Some people don't like to consider the increased power granted with a promotion, because they feel that power is undesirable. People who are powerful are somehow to be feared and disliked, and aspiring to gain power isn't considered honorable. This is because the type of power that paternalism has spawned is coercive. It is power *over* others. Power in a loving organization is principle-centered; that is, it is based on a fair and ethical philosophy. It is used to influence others rather than to control or manipulate them. It is used to carry out philosophies while keeping the good of the organization, customers, employees, self, and society in mind. By hiring and promoting leaders who practice principle-centered management and wield principal-centered power, an organization can more quickly increase its loving leadership quotient.

Companies with high quotients have established human-resources practices that follow through on their management philosophies. At a minimum, these practices should include employee safety, employee recognition, employee development, and an employee assistance program. Written policies should be kept to the smallest possible number, but those necessary to a maternalistic environment include expectations for teamwork, customer service, communication systems, interpersonal relations, and continuous quality improvement. There will also be the more mundane policies that almost every organization develops (e.g., dress code, absenteeism, and leave of absence procedures).

Personnel policies, along with the mission statement, philosophy, and job descriptions and standards, are a reflection of what an organization values. A quality operation values quality. That means quality in its products, quality service to customers, quality work life for employees, and quality management and leadership. Implicit in quality are standards for all of these areas. These standards define minimum requirements and behaviors. Maternalistic managers require quality standards to be met, and they intervene when they are not.

Examples of Personnel Policies for the
Maternalistic Organization

Employee Assistance

An employee in trouble (with money problems, substance abuse, marital problems, etc.) has a defined place to go for help and counseling.

Employee Recognition

There are rewards, celebrations, and recognition activities for milestones, accomplishments, and growth.

Employee Safety

The company has active programs to keep everyone safe at work: protected from injury, violence, harassment, etc.

Employee Productivity

The company encourages work breaks for stressed associates, including such things as afternoon walks outside and short naps at work.

Customer Service

Employees are held accountable for service, including basic common courtesy.

CQI

Everyone has accountability for quality and for working to improve it.

Empowerment

Everyone is empowered to do their jobs to the best of their ability, to take risks, and to provide service to others.

Every individual makes choices every day. The choices made by leaders are indicative of what they value. Valuing the organization leads to choices, as in the examples that follow, that ensure the organization's survival, whether these be in the strategic (big picture) or the operational arena.

Examples of Choices That Indicate a Valuing of the Organization

Choosing to reward teamwork and to be intolerant of turf building within the company.

Choosing to celebrate and reward growth in others (e.g., educational accomplishments, the completion of a difficult new task).

Choosing to reward quality work and to be intolerant of shoddiness or lack of quality.

Choosing to make decisions for the good of the entire organization rather than just one's own department.

Choosing to make decisions for the long-term thriving of the company rather than for short-term quick wins.

Choosing to encourage, reward, protect, and recognize the creativity of associates.

The choices made regarding personnel indicate a valuing or lack of valuing of the people (sometimes called "human resources") within the company. Still other choices indicate how the customers and the self are valued, as in the examples that follow.

Examples of Choices That Indicate a Valuing of Work Associates

Choosing to encourage, provide opportunities for, and invest in programs for lifelong learning—for every employee.

Choosing to share information with associates, including choosing to trust them with financial numbers.

Choosing to help employees lead a balanced life by not expecting mandatory overtime, and by offering such things as exercise classes, flexible scheduling, on-site child and elder care, classes on stress reduction, parenting, and time management, and an on-site occupational-health nurse.

Choosing to promote from within (even if an internal candidate will need additional training that an external candidate may already have).

Choosing to openly address current problems, such as violence in the workplace, with plans to detect potential problems and prevent/ protect from them.

Choosing to empower by giving necessary work tools and then *getting out of the way,* so that others can do their jobs without bureaucratic interference.

I ask people in interviews what their personal values are. They stop and ask "Why, what do you mean by that?"

– Thomas Kuczmarski, writer

Examples of Choices That Indicate a Valuing of Customers

Choosing to elicit feedback from customers about what they want, and then acting on that feedback.

Choosing to reward customer service and to be intolerant of less-than-exceptional service.

Choosing to provide a service or product that is of value to the customer, and refusing to make profit more important than safe, ethical, high-quality products.

Choosing to be honest in advertising and marketing and not to promise more than can be delivered.

Choosing to employ only a competent team. Correcting incompetence with education, the enforcement of standards, and, *if necessary,* discipline (including termination).

Examples of Choices That Indicate a Valuing of Self

Choosing to invest in continuing education and lifelong learning for yourself.

Choosing not to work excessively long hours but to balance work with the rest of life: family, friends, hobbies, leisure time.

Choosing to maintain good health through diet, exercise, medical checkups, and maintaining an appropriate weight.

Choosing not to stay in a "toxic" environment, or in an organization where the culture and ethics don't match your own.

Choosing personal rewards and celebrations for yourself when goals are met or successes occur.

All of the written protocols in the world mean nothing if the behavior doesn't match the philosophy. Theories, no matter how grand or appealing, are not the real world. Actions are the reality. What leaders *do*, every hour of every day, demonstrates both their values and their level of commitment. The current state of affairs in many organizations indicates that high values and high levels of commitment are not widespread among the people Americans call bosses. The following are examples of ways for loving leaders to demonstrate their commitment to excellence.

Some Common-Sense Actions That Indicate Values

Handwritten thank-you notes to associates, colleagues, customers, bosses, and others when some kind of acknowledgment is appropriate. The message should be: "I noticed what you did, and I appreciate you."

The solicitation of feedback from everyone (customers, colleagues, "subordinates") about the company and the boss's performance, which feedback is then welcomed, listened to, and evaluated— *never* rejected without analysis, greeted with defensiveness, or punished.

True "open door" behavior by leaders who answer their own telephones, visit worksites, and welcome approaches and/or questions from everyone.

Polite, respectful communication to everyone.

Company-sponsored celebrations or ceremonies to honor associates who have met company *or* personal goals (example: a college degree).

Yes, there are leaders everywhere who want to see change in their companies. That's why so many embrace new management theories with the eager anticipation that "this will be the one that turns everything around." They fail to understand that it is their own common sense, combined with love, that can make the difference in their companies.

The term "maternalism" has been used in this book to describe a loving way of leading. The concept is based on encouraging growth and development for everyone in the company. It is neither manipulative nor neglectful, in that it sets the degree of management control according to organizational and individual maturity levels. It describes a management style characterized by strong leaders who use their station to bring out the best in others. If adopted as an organization-wide philosophy, maternalism will create the passion necessary for a thriving enterprise.

In medicine, the term "psychoneuroimmunology" refers to the interaction between the brain, the endocrine system, and the immune system. The word is used to describe the degree to which belief *becomes* biology. What the brain thinks can affect what the body secretes internally and how well it can fight disease. Similarly, in management we could coin the term "psychoneuromanagement," because—whatever leadership tools or techniques we use—it is what we think, believe, and value that controls our interactions and determines how strong the organization will be.

Organizational leaders in the best organizations are, and will be in the future, those who balance the needs of the company, the customers, the workers, and themselves.

Slighting any one of these causes an imbalance that limits the future for all.

Managers and organizations have a choice. They can continue to choose behaviors based on paternalism. They can enthusiastically adopt new management techniques and then abandon them when the newest "latest-greatest" idea comes along. Or they can work to increase their maternalistic quotients. "Bosses" today have a lot of challenges ahead of them, but there is, and always will be, a need for leaders who are willing to meet these problems head-on. The ability to do this, and do it well, will require wisdom, courage, and—most of all—love.

*I*ndex

Order Form

CALL TOLL-FREE: (888) 895-2036
Please have your credit card available.

MAIL this form to Vashon Publishing
P.O. Box 510, Olalla, WA 98359

FAX this form to (360) 876-1952

ONLINE: Visit us in cyberspace
at: www.vashonpublishing.com

Please send me _____ copies of *Leading
With Love*. Enclosed is $23.95 per book. $ _____

Washington residents add 8.1% sales tax $ _____

Shipping and handling: $4.00 for the first
book plus $2.00 for each additional book $ _____

Total: $ _____

Mail to: _____

_____

_____

_____

❑ Enclosed is my check   Please bill my:
❑ Visa   ❑ MasterCard

Credit card # _____

Name on card _____ Exp. _____

Please call to find out about discounts for orders over 10 books.

Thank you!